May God bless you on your journey of faith!

Love,
Heather M.

July 2014

A Journey of Faith:
Lessons Learned in the Fire

H EATHER M C C ORMICK

CROSSBOOKS

CrossBooks™
A Division of LifeWay
1663 Liberty Drive
Bloomington, IN 47403
www.crossbooks.com
Phone: 1-866-879-0502

Scripture taken from the Holman Christian Standard Bible ® Copyright © 2003, 2002, 2000, 1999 by Holman Bible Publishers. All rights reserved.

First published by CrossBooks 06/09/2014

ISBN: 978-1-4627-3717-8 (sc)
ISBN: 978-1-4627-3719-2 (hc)
ISBN: 978-1-4627-3718-5 (e)

Library of Congress Control Number: 2014908352

Printed in the United States of America.

This book is printed on acid-free paper.

Acknowledgements

Praise to the Father, the God of all comfort and the Father of compassion! He never left me. He loved me, and He encouraged me every step of the way.

Thanks to my husband Lionel; without his love and support this book would not be possible. Thank you, Lionel, for encouraging me through the trials that we faced together. I love you!

Thanks also to my parents, who lovingly raised me in a Christian home, who taught me God's truths, and who have encouraged and prayed for me throughout my life. Thank you, Mom, for being my editor and proofreader.

Finally, thank you to all who prayed for us on this journey of faith. Your support, your encouragement, and your prayers have been very meaningful to us!

Contents

Introduction

Infertility. It is an issue that no couple wants to face, yet statistics state that as many as 10.9% of American women (6.7 million women) experience difficulties in becoming pregnant or carrying a baby to term.[1] I found myself as one of these statistics. Thus began my journey of faith, one that included not only struggling with infertility but also grieving the losses of loved ones, becoming a caregiver for a loved one, and hurting over disagreements within my family.

This journey of faith included many emotions such as frustration, hurt, anxiety, grief, and despair. I struggled as I learned new medical terms. Complex decisions which related to not only my own health but also the health of my father-in-law confronted me. I mourned the losses of loved ones, and I rejoiced in unexpected blessings.

My journey has been long and hard; it was unexpected and at times unwelcomed. However, God has been faithful every minute of every day. He has brought me through the struggles and has taught me many lessons along the way.

My Dear Reader, this book chronicles the journey of faith on which God led me, and it describes the lessons that He taught me along the way. While I had many hesitations related to writing about my experiences, I want to share with you all that God has taught me. My prayer is that no matter what struggles you are facing, reading what God has done in my life will uplift you. I pray that the lessons which God has taught me will encourage you. However, my greatest hope is that this book will point you to God because this book is about Him and what He has done. I want God to be honored. He deserves it!

This book is divided by the lessons that I learned (and am still learning). Some lessons you will see more than once because God reinforced those lessons again and again. Use this book as a devotional, or search through it to find the lesson(s) that will encourage you the most in your personal journey of faith. Then venture to the back of the book, and use the questions and Scriptures included there for further reflection on each lesson. May God teach and inspire you along the way!

Lesson 1

Answered Prayers

My journey of faith began with a question, "God, should my husband and I have children?" This seems like such an unassuming question because the answer for most married couples is "yes." My husband Lionel and I had been happily married for over five years without children, and we were quite content with our life as it was. We experienced success in our careers; Lionel was an accountant, and I taught mathematics at a local community college. Church, family, friends, and work filled our lives. God had truly blessed us. However, the question of children kept nagging at me. One day this question weighed particularly heavily on my mind. The change that a little one would bring frightened me; but I kept wondering, "What if we had children? Would that be the right decision or the wrong one?" As my students were testing that day, I kept praying and praying, seeking God's direction. The answer came, in an unexpected way, but God showed Lionel and me that having children was His will for our lives. God had heard and answered my prayer for direction.

The book of Psalms contains many reassurances about God's hearing and answering our prayers. Psalm 3 reads, "I cry aloud to the Lord, and He answers me from His holy mountain" (Ps. 3:4). Psalm 4 mentions how God hears our prayers when we call out to Him (Ps 4:3). In Psalm 5 David, one of the psalmists, states that God hears his voice at daybreak and that he waits expectantly for God's answer (Ps. 5:3). Psalm 6 tells how God listens to our pleas and accepts our prayers (Ps.

6:9). Psalm 10 says, "Lord, You have heard the desire of the humble; You will strengthen their hearts. You will listen carefully" (Ps. 10:17). These reassurances of answered prayers occur in the first ten psalms, and there are 140 more psalms that continue to proclaim God's goodness and His responsiveness to our prayers.

Psalms is not the only book in the Old Testament that records answered prayers; these answers appear throughout the Old Testament. Hannah prays for a child, and God gives her Samuel (1 Sam. 1–2). Solomon asks God for wisdom, and God blesses him with wisdom renown throughout Israel and many other nations (1 Kings 3–4). On Mount Carmel Elijah asks God to reveal Himself to the people of Israel as the one true God. God answers by sending fire down from heaven to burn up the sacrifice on the altar, a sacrifice drenched with water (1 Kings 18). Hezekiah asks God for healing, and God heals him (Isa. 38). Jonah calls to God from the belly of a big fish, and God causes the fish to spit Jonah out on dry land (Jonah 1–2). These are just a few of the many examples of answered prayers found in the Old Testament.

The New Testament, too, refers to God's answers to prayers. In Matthew at least twice Jesus assures His disciples that God will answer their prayers (Matt. 18:19–20; 21:21–22). Hebrews 4:16 states, "Therefore let us approach the throne of grace with boldness, so that we may receive mercy and find grace to help us at the proper time." John also writes about having confidence before God because we know that He hears us (1 John 5:14–15). These passages are further promises of answered prayers, and the New Testament includes many other such references.

My Dear Reader, as you can see, the Bible is full of assurances that God always listens to and answers our prayer. His answer may be "yes", it may be "no", or it may be "wait." His answers may not be what you expect or even what you want, but He always answers when we call.

LESSON 2

When There Seems To Be No Answer

The Bible is full of assurances that God answers prayers, though sometimes when we pray we do not seem to get an answer. Lionel and I have prayed and prayed for a child, but God has not yet granted our request. Many times I have wondered why God has not given us a child. Have I been praying for the wrong thing? Have I been praying for the wrong reasons? Am I being too impatient? Do I have enough faith? I have even wondered sometimes if my prayers are futile and are lifted up in vain. The waiting and the silence have been extremely challenging and frustrating; however, through these God has taught me to examine myself. He reminded me that there are several reasons for seemingly unanswered prayers.

If your prayer seems unanswered, maybe you have not actually talked to God about your need, your desire, or your concern. James writes, "You desire and do not have. You murder and covet and cannot obtain. You fight and war. You do not have because you do not ask" (James 4:2). If your prayer seems unanswered, think for a moment about the following questions. Have you prayed to God? Have you talked to Him about your need or your desire? Yes, God knows our needs and our wants before we ask Him, but He also wants us to talk to Him. This is what builds our relationship with Him. Just as you develop a friendship with a person by spending time with him or her, our relationship with God grows when we spend time with Him and talk to Him. Tell God what you need or want; He cannot answer if you do not pray.

If your prayer seems unanswered, maybe your motives are wrong. James also pens these words, "You ask and do not receive because you ask with wrong motives, so that you may spend it on your evil desires" (James 4:3). Have you ever asked God for clothes, shoes, a house, a car, a… (fill in the blank with what you want)? Did you ask Him because you truly needed it, or did you ask Him because you wanted it? Did you ask Him so that you would be "blessed", or did you ask so that you could be a blessing to others?

At times we do not seem to get an answer because we have not asked others to pray with us. In Matthew 18:19 – 20 Jesus tells His disciples that if several of them are praying together about an issue, God will answer. You do not need to share your request with the whole world, but do get a couple of trusted friends to pray with you and for you. I asked friends and family to pray for Lionel and me many times during this journey of faith. The prayers of these loved ones made our struggles a little easier. Realizing how many people cared about us and our child encouraged us, and God used the prayers of others to comfort us when the hurt was great and to strengthen us when our faith was weak. Now we look forward to celebrating with our family and friends however God chooses to answer our prayers.

Sometimes we do not seem to get an answer because what we are not praying is not God's will. Praying God's will is vital in having our prayers answered. First John 5:14 – 15 tells us that we can have confidence when we pray according to God's will because God will hear and answer us. So how do you know you are praying God's will? First, ask God to guide your prayers and to show you how to pray. I cannot tell you how many times I have asked God to show me how to pray. Sometimes He led me to pray in the same way I had been praying, and sometimes He showed me that my prayer and/or my attitude needed adjusting to fall in line with what He wanted rather than what I wanted. Second, search God's Word to know if you are praying God's will. His Word is His will; and if you pray verses from the Bible, then you can know for sure that you are praying God's will. If your prayers seem unanswered, I encourage you to examine your prayers. Are you praying according to God's will? Are you willing to accept a "no" or a "not yet" from Him?

Finally, sometimes we do not seem to receive an answer to our prayer because we do not believe. When James writes about asking for wisdom (James 1:5), he also states that we should ask with faith and that a doubter should not expect his prayers to be answered (James 1:6–7). Are you praying out of habit because praying is what Christians are supposed to do? Or are you praying in faith, believing that God will hear and answer?

The gospel of Matthew tells the following story about Jesus near the end of His life. When Jesus is on His way back to Jerusalem after spending the night in Bethany, He is hungry and sees a fig tree, only there are no figs on the tree. Jesus says to the fig tree, "May you never have fruit again!" and immediately the fig tree withers. The disciples noticing what has happened are astounded (just as we would be) and probably stand with their jaws dropped in surprise, mouths wide open (Matt. 21:18–20). Jesus answers their astonishment with these words, "I assure you: If you have faith and do not doubt, you will not only do what was done to the fig tree, but even if you tell this mountain, 'Be lifted up and thrown into the sea,' it will be done. And if you believe, you will receive whatever you ask for in prayer" (Matt. 21:21–22).

Notice the last part of what Jesus says, "And if you believe, you will receive whatever you ask for in prayer." Do you truly believe that God is listening to you? Do you truly believe He will answer? Faith is not always easy; in fact, it has been one of my biggest struggles over the last few years. To keep praying and to keep believing is hard when you do not see immediate answers to your prayers. However, do not give up because God promises to answer when we pray and believe. Remember that God's ways are not our ways; they are much better than ours (Isa. 55:8–9). Also do not forget that God's timing is much better than ours. Ask and believe that God will answer. Ask and look for God's answer—be it "yes", "no", or "wait."

My Dear Reader, as Hebrews 4:16 encourages us, approach God with confidence (and with humility and a willingness to submit to Him). He is merciful and loving. Pour out your heart to Him. He is listening and He promises to answer! He will give you the grace and the help that you need.

LESSON 3

The God of All Comfort

Shortly after Lionel and I decided to move forward with having children, I got sick, nothing severe or lasting, but my illness delayed our plans for children. I was extremely discouraged and upset by this. We were so excited about our dream of having children that waiting a while longer was a bitter disappointment. In fact, as I got out of my car after work one afternoon, I was crying. Our neighbor's dog came into our garage about that time. She seemed happy to see me because she was wagging her tail. I petted her for a bit; and as I did so, I began to feel emotionally better. I thought to myself, "Well, maybe waiting a bit won't be so bad." God sent my neighbor's dog over just when I needed the comfort and encouragement that only a pet can deliver. God, being the God of all comfort, knew what type of comfort I needed at that moment.

2 Corinthians 1:3 – 4 are some of my favorite verses. This passage says, "Praise the God and Father of our Lord Jesus Christ, the Father of mercies and the God of all comfort. He comforts us in all our affliction, so that we may be able to comfort those who are in any kind of affliction, through the comfort we ourselves receive from God." Did you catch that? God is the Father of mercies; He sees your struggles, and He has compassion on you. He is the God of all comfort so He reaches out to comfort you when you hurt. Maybe He puts a song on the radio to soothe you; maybe you get a note from a friend who reminds you that she is praying for you. Maybe He leads you to a particular passage

in His Word that encourages you, or maybe someone just gives you a compliment that brightens your day. No matter what your struggle, God knows and understands your pain. He hurts with you. He cries with you. He never, ever leaves you. He meets you where you are, and He reaches out to comfort you. He loves you! Do not ever doubt that!

However, do not miss the second part of 2 Corinthians 1:3 – 4; God comforts us so that we can comfort others. You are not the only one who hurts. You are not the only one who struggles. God can use the storms that you have faced to help you encourage others who may be in similar situations. I cannot tell you how many times this has been true in my life. After I have struggled, healed, and found strength in God, I have been able to counsel and comfort others who are facing trials similar to the fires through which I have passed. God has given me words to say to them that will be wise and encouraging because I have been in their shoes. He has also helped me pray for them; I know better how to pray because I have been in a comparable circumstance.

My Dear Reader, when you are hurting, look to God; He is the Father of mercies and the God of all comfort. Then as He heals and strengthens you, be a willing vessel and allow Him to use you to minister to others and to bless them. Reaching out to others, even when we are hurting, can sometimes be part of the healing process. Is there someone whom you need to comfort and/or encourage?

LESSON 4

Pouring Out Your Heart

I mentioned in Lesson 1 that God answered my prayers for direction, but I did not tell you how He answered. One of my older students, whom I respected and who had become a friend, had a dream that I was pregnant; and she shared this dream with me. The next semester this same student came back to my office, telling me about another dream she had. In this dream I experienced pregnancy complications, but I and our baby boy were healthy. Little did this student realize that once again she was an answer to my prayer. I had been struggling that week with the "what ifs", the biggest of which was "What if I miscarry?" I was extremely worried about a miscarriage, and I had been praying and talking to God about my concerns.

Psalm 62:8 says, "Trust in Him at all times, you people; pour out your hearts before Him. God is our refuge." Tell God what is troubling you. Are you hurting? Express your hurts to Him. He is the Great Physician; He heals our physical hurts, as well as our emotional hurts. Are you angry? Talk to Him about your anger, even if that anger is directed at Him. He will help you let go of the anger and forgive. Are you confused? Tell Him and ask for direction. He will give you the reassurance and the direction that you need. Are you full of questions? Ask God the questions: the "what ifs" and the "whys"; then trust Him with the answers. Do not go pulling the questions back into your mind; leave the questions and their answers in God's hands. Be honest with God; He is big enough to handle your questions and your emotions, and He will help you sort through these. (Please do not get me wrong; when I encourage you to ask God the questions that are in your mind and to express your emotions to Him, I am not saying that you should go ranting and raving against Him or even to Him. After all, He is the God Almighty, the Creator of the universe, the Sovereign God, and the Holy One. Make no mistake; we are to fear Him. This means that while we are to be honest with Him, we should approach Him with awe and with respect.)

Pouring out your heart to God not only involves telling Him about your concerns, but it also entails expressing your joys to Him. Praise and thank Him for what He has done for you, especially when He answers your prayers. Rejoice with Him over the good that happens in your life. We have so much for which to be thankful. We have so much over which to rejoice. God has blessed us!

My Dear Reader, pour out your heart to God. God already knows what is in your heart, but part of having a relationship with Him is talking to Him and sharing with Him what is on your mind—both good and bad. He is always listening, and He gives you His full attention. He loves you!

LESSON 5

Working for Our Good

I mentioned in the previous lesson that I had been pouring out my heart to God, expressing to Him my worry about miscarrying a baby. I also told you that God answered my concern through the dream of a friend. God used this dream to remind me that no matter what happens in my life, He has a bigger plan. Even when we hurt and even when we do not understand why circumstances happen the way they do, God always knows and does what is best for us.

This is a lesson of which God must frequently remind me. Life gets tough, and I forget that God is still in control. I begin to have a pity party, to focus on myself, and to lose sight of God. I often have to remember two particular verses from the Bible that address God's work for our good: Jeremiah 29:11 and Romans 8:28. The first verse states, "For I know the plans I have for you'—this is the Lord's declaration—'plans for your welfare, not for disaster, to give you a future and a hope.'" The second Scripture continues this thought, "We know that all things work together for the good of those who love God: those who are called according to His purpose." Did you catch that? God knows what plans He has for you, plans that are for your good. His plans are to help you, not to harm you. He plans to give you hope and a future. Yes, the road may get tough, and you may hit some potholes along the way. However, God promises to work everything that happens in your life for your good. This may not seem to materialize right away, but God is often working in ways that we do not see or do not fully understand.

I need to mention, though, that the promise of God's working everything for our good has two qualifiers with it. One, this promise is for those who love God, for those who have chosen to follow Him. Two, this promise is for those whom God has called and for those who are obeying that call. If you are stubbornly doing what you want to do, regardless of whether or not God says your actions are right, not everything will work out for good.

As long as I have been obeying God, every struggle that I have faced in my life, including dealing with infertility, has always worked out for the best. I do not understand all of the hurts that I have endured, but I do know that God has used each one to make me a better woman, a woman who (while I still have a long way yet to go) looks a little more like Him. He taught me lessons (some of which I am sharing with you now) that I might not have learned any other way or that might not have "stuck" any other way. Beyond that, I have been able to help others who are facing similar trials. No, the hurt was not easy to endure, but I cannot deny God's work through the fires that I have faced—His work for the best.

I do not know what struggle you are currently facing, but I can promise you that if you love Him and follow Him, God is working for your good even through the bad things that happen. Turn to Him, and recognize that He always knows and does what is best. My Dear Reader, trust Him; there is no better way to walk through life than with the Lord.

LESSON 6

God Is in Control

As my student shared her second dream with me (see Lesson 4), I realized that God has a bigger plan even if that design includes struggles along the way. We may not always understand His blueprint, but God is in control of all that happens. Some circumstances He causes; others He allows. Either way, our lives are in His hands no matter what happens. We may try to make our own choices, to follow our own plans, and to control our own destinies. However, there is never a minute when He is not in control. We may not like the situations in which we find ourselves, but at those times we can still know that God is sovereign. Rather than fighting God or running away from Him, we need to pour out our hearts to Him, to trust Him, and to submit to Him. When faced with troubling circumstances, we need to ask ourselves, "Is this a situation that I caused by doing what was wrong, or has God allowed this problem to teach me? Am I trying to control my own life, or am I following God?"

Psalm 33:11 says, "The counsel of the Lord stands firm forever, the plans of His heart from generation to generation." Proverbs 19:21 confirms this, "Many plans are in a man's heart, but the Lord's decree will prevail." And Proverbs 16:4 states, "The Lord has prepared everything for His purpose—even the wicked for the day of disaster." Do not miss this lesson! Sometimes when the world seems to be spinning hysterically and there is absolutely nothing you can do about it, you may wonder, "Is there anyone who is in control?" The answer to that question is yes!

Absolutely, positively yes! God knows what happens every minute of every day; He is sovereign over each circumstance in our lives. There is absolutely nothing that He cannot handle.

When I was in college, Twila Paris came out with the song "God Is in Control." The words of the song declare that we do not need to be afraid or discouraged because no matter what happens God is still in control. We can rest in Him, focus on Him, and hold onto Him because He will never forsake us and because He will never fail or disappoint us. He watches over us and no power compares to His.[1]

How true and timely this song is! There is never a minute that God is not in control. He is never sleeping and never caught off guard. He never quits paying attention and He never slips up. His plans stand firm forever. His purpose prevails. He works out everything according to His good plan. God will never make a mistake or miss a detail. He has everything under control. Heaven and earth and all that happens in them are under His dominion (Job 25:2; Ps. 22:28).

My Dear Reader, your times are in God's hands (Ps. 31:15); rest in that promise.

LESSON 7

Parents Must Be Intentional

O ne day I was walking for exercise and praying while I walked. As I prayed, God impressed upon me that our child would be a very special child. I had no idea, however, how special the birth of this child would be. I did not realize the loss we would face, the time we would have to wait, and the numerous prayers that family, friends, and we would lift up in the meantime. I realize that each child is special and is a gift from God, but the impression God gave me was a different one—a foreshadowing, so to speak, of the journey to come. I also sensed that God would use our child in a special way, and this meant that Lionel and I would have to be conscientious about raising our child in God's ways.

Deuteronomy 6:6 – 7 reminds us of the importance of intentionally teaching our children God's ways: "These words that I am giving you today are to be in your heart. Repeat them to your children. Talk about them when you sit in your house and when you walk along the road, when you lie down and when you get up." Did you get that? God's commands are to be in our hearts, and more than that we are to repeat them to our children. This means that we are to intentionally teach our children about God. So how can we do that? Notice the next part of the passage. "Talk about them when you sit in your house and when you walk along the road, when you lie down and when you get up." Maybe we do not walk along the road any more, but the connotation is still there. Talk about God, His love, and His Word every chance you get—not just at church. Yes, children will learn about God at church, but the lessons do not need to just come on Sunday mornings, Sunday nights, and/or Wednesday nights. The lessons need to be daily, and parents are responsible for ensuring that their children learn about God.

One way to do this is to seek opportunities to talk about God to your children, and make the most of these chances. If your child notices a beautiful flower or is fascinated by animals, remind him/her that God created those. Suppose your teenager is hurt by the words or actions of a friend; speak to him/her about forgiveness and how God has forgiven us. If your son is anxious about an upcoming test, pray with him. Suppose your daughter is watching something questionable on television, remind her of God's values. Pray with your children in the morning when they wake up, and pray with them again at night when they go to bed. Share with them what God is doing in your life, and teach them to notice God's work in their lives.

My Dear Reader, look for teachable moments with your children and seize them!

LESSON 8

Christians as Ambassadors

A s God impressed upon me the importance of intentionally teaching our future child about Him, He also reminded me of other children in my life and how I am to be a godly example to them too. In fact, God calls us to be ambassadors for Him wherever we go to whomever we meet (2 Cor. 5:20), He challenges us to intentionally live out our faith, and He encourages us to make the most of opportunities that He gives us.

Since people are always watching what you do and their ears are listening to what you say, think for a few minutes about these questions. Are you a good ambassador for God, appropriately representing Him (2 Cor. 5:20)? Does your light shine before people and point to God (Matt. 5:16)? Are your words honoring to God? Is your conversation full of grace (Col. 4:6)? Is your life pure, radiating Jesus' love through your actions? Do you talk about God often? Do you tell others what He has done for you?

The above questions refer to ways that we can be ambassadors for God, but the Bible is our best guide to being God's representative. Deuteronomy 6:7 – 9 states, "Talk about them when you sit in your house and when you walk along the road, when you lie down and when you get up. Bind them as a sign on your hand and let them be a symbol on your forehead. Write them on the doorposts of your house and on your gates." Notice how often the Israelites were to speak of and to see God's commands: at home, along the road, on their hands, on their foreheads, on the doorframes of their houses, and on their gates. This was everywhere they went; God's commands were to saturate their lives. Is your life soaked in God's Word? Do you read and study it each day? You need to interact with God's Word more than just at church. Dive into it and let it inundate your life. Learn it; seek to understand it. You should not just read the Bible to mark this activity off your Christian to-do list. Spend quality time getting your hands and heart in it and all over it. If you devote time to God's Word each day—reading it, studying it, meditating on it, and then listening to see what God says to you through it—you will be better prepared to be God's ambassador. You will not be able to help speaking of God and His Word, and you will be more likely to live by His ways.

My Dear Reader, my challenge to you is to spend time with God, saturate your life in Him, and allow Him to become your passion; then you cannot help but talk about Him. Pray for your eyes to open to opportunities to speak of Him; then look for those openings and seize them. There is a world that needs to hear of God's love so be intentional in living out your faith. Be an ambassador for Christ.

LESSON 9

Draw Close Together

Throughout the last couple of years, Lionel and I faced many fires, including losing both my grandfather and Lionel's dad, dealing with infertility and the resulting treatments, and being financially pinched due to the costs of fertility tests and treatments. However, through each trial we faced, we shared our hurts and our disappointments with each other rather than withdrawing from each other. We talked about our struggles, we prayed together, and we encouraged and supported each other through the detours and over the potholes that were in our path. This has strengthened our marriage and led us to a deeper intimacy. At times we were both "down" and we hurt together. More often, God graciously would allow one of us to be "up" while the other was "down" so that we were able to encourage and comfort each other.

I have heard a saying about marriage: "Your sorrows are halved and your joys are doubled." Your sorrows are halved because you have someone who shares them with you. This does not lessen the ache, but knowing that someone hurts with you takes some of the sting out of the pain. While for some people withdrawing is a natural reaction when you are hurting, do not withdraw from your spouse. God intends for you to help and support each other. Remember that God made Eve to be a helper or a helpmate (depending on which translation of Genesis 2 you read) for Adam. God intends the same today for a husband and wife. Share your hurts and your burdens. Be honest with each other but do so in love. Talk to your mate but also take time to listen. Pray for each other; and pray together over the problems, hurts, and struggles you face.

My Dear Reader, life hurts; it always has and always will. I know that is not encouraging to read; but as long as we are on this side of heaven, we live in a fallen world and pain is a part of that world. Look to God first to help you with that hurt. Pour out your heart to Him. Then talk to your spouse, share your feelings honestly and lovingly, and pray together. Let your pain draw you and your spouse closer together and into a deeper intimacy with each other. Do not let it drive a wedge between you.

LESSON 10

God's Perfect Timing

When we lost my grandfather Peewee, my post on Facebook was as follows: "Today the world lost a great man. My grandfather passed away this morning." That statement described both my feelings and Peewee's life. Peewee had lived a long and full life, positively influencing many people; and my heart ached after his death. I was the apple of his eye and he had been the apple of mine.

At the time of Peewee's death, Lionel and I had been praying for a child, but I was not pregnant and I did not understand why. However, when Peewee passed away, I began to understand a small piece of God's timing. Had I been pregnant at the time, the emotions following Peewee's death would not have been good for the baby or for me.

Ecclesiastes 3:11 says, "He has made everything appropriate in its time. He has also put eternity in their hearts, but man cannot discover the work God has done from beginning to end." My Dear Reader, never doubt that God knows what He is doing. His timing is impeccable because He sees the bigger picture while we see only a piece of the puzzle. We may not understand why or when things happen, but God does. He has a plan, His plan is always good and His timing is perfect. He uses each season of our lives (even periods of grief) to make us better and to help us look a little more like Him.

Lionel and I did not marry until I was nearly 30 years old, and waiting for the right man stretched my patience, but a praise and worship song encouraged me during that period of my life. Maybe I should have sung this song more while waiting for a child. The song is entitled "In His Time." It reminds us that God makes everything beautiful and He always keeps His promises, but that these happen only in His perfect timing. The song challenges us to praise God, to trust Him, and to wait on Him.[1]

Remember God will make everything beautiful and appropriate in His time (Eccl. 3:11); we just have to trust His perfect timing even when He says, "Wait."

LESSON 11

Heaven

B ecause I was so close to my grandfather, his death crushed me. I treasured the time that I had spent with him, and I knew that I would miss him tremendously. In the midst of my grief, God reminded me of the promise of heaven; consequently, I recognized that my grandfather was in heaven, that he was whole again and no longer suffered from Parkinson's disease, and that one day I would see him again.

In John 14:1 – 3 Jesus says to His disciples, "Your heart must not be troubled. Believe in God; believe also in Me. In My Father's house are many dwelling places; if not, I would have told you. I am going away to prepare a place for you. If I go away and prepare a place for you, I will come back and receive you to Myself, so that where I am you may be also." I am getting excited now just thinking about Jesus' words. What an awesome promise this is! One day Jesus will take us to be with Him!

I used to get impatient for heaven because I was tired of the hurts of this life. I knew heaven would be great because there would be no pain there, and I was looking forward to not ever crying again (Rev. 21:4). However, recently I have come to realize that heaven is so much more than that. Heaven is where God is and I can only imagine how that will be. I eagerly wait for Jesus to take me to be with Him. I long to never have to leave His presence, to be where He is 24/7, and to never again have sin hinder my relationship with Him. Oh, how marvelous!

Heaven could be the worst dump (by the way, it's not!), but it would still be heaven because of God.

Revelation 21 – 22 describes heaven, also called the Holy City or the New Jerusalem. Heaven will shine with the brilliance of God, brilliance like that of jewels. In fact, God's glory will be so bright that there will be no sun or moon. The Holy City will have a magnificent wall with twelve gates of pearl and twelve foundations of jewels. Its streets will be of pure gold and the river of the water of life will flow through the middle of the city. Beside the river will be the tree of life bearing twelve crops each year. Nothing impure will enter New Jerusalem. There will be no temple in the city because God is its temple. God's throne will be in heaven and we will serve Him. God's name will be on our foreheads and we will see His face (Rev. 21:9–22:5). My Dear Reader, did you catch that last part? We will see God's face! Can you imagine beholding God in all of His glory, in all of His splendor, and in all of His holiness? What a sight that will be!

Wow! What more can I say? I cannot wait! I fully understand Paul's struggle, "For me, living is Christ and dying is gain. Now if I live on in the flesh, this means fruitful work for me; and I do not know which one I should choose. I am pressured by both. I have the desire to depart and be with Christ—which is far better—but to remain in the flesh is more necessary for you" (Phil. 1:21–24). I long for heaven, but I know that God has a plan for me in the here and now. So in the meantime, I will choose to serve Him and to wait eagerly for the day that He takes me home to Him.

LESSON 12

The God of All Comfort

I know that I have already mentioned this lesson, but reminding both you and me never hurts. In fact, many of the lessons I "learned" through the fire were lessons that I had already been taught; I just needed to remember them.

The week after my grandfather Peewee died, I struggled tremendously. My heart was broken. I often wept before God and told Him how much I missed my granddaddy. On one particular day as I was playing my keyboard and crying, God gave me a vision that I do not think I will ever forget. Before his death Peewee had Parkinson's disease which made him shake. Eating and walking were difficult for him, and at times his speech was slurred. In the vision God gave me, I saw a glimpse of my grandfather in heaven, and in that glimpse I knew he was whole and healed. Peewee was ageless and was standing tall, as I had not seen him stand for a while. My faith had been shaken because believing both that Peewee was in heaven and that one day Lionel and I would have a child was almost too much for me, but through this vision God gave me the reassurance I needed. From that moment on, I was comforted. Yes, I still missed my grandfather, and yes, I still cried in my grief; but healing began. Only God could have known exactly what I needed. Only God could have given me that vision and the reassurance and comfort that came with it.

God knows your hurts, your worries, your concerns, and your grief. He cares and He hurts for you. John 11:35 is a simple verse, "Jesus wept."

Lazarus dies and Jesus comes to Bethany to see his sisters. When Jesus sees their grief, He is moved by it (John 11:33) and He weeps. I do not think Jesus is weeping because Lazarus is dead. Jesus knows that He will raise Lazarus from the dead; in fact, earlier He had told His disciples that Lazarus had fallen asleep and that He is going to wake him (John 11:11). I think Jesus is crying because He sees how deeply His friends hurt over Lazarus' death. In the same way, I believe that because Jesus loves us, He weeps with us when we hurt and when we grieve. He reaches out to us and He comforts us. Sometimes He gives us an overwhelming sense of His presence. Sometimes He points us to just the right Scripture to encourage us. Sometimes He sends a friend to encourage us. Sometimes He plays song on the radio to soothe us. Jesus knows how to best comfort you and He does.

When I was in college, Scott Krippayne sang a song entitled "Sometimes He Calms the Storm." The song describes a storm in the life of a Christian. Problems seem to swirl all around, and everything appears out of control. Sometimes God brings the problems to an end, but other times He has lessons to teach us. At those times rather than bringing an outward peace in the form of no struggles or hurts, He brings us an inward peace, a peace in our hearts that surpasses our understanding (Phil. 4:7).[1]

My Dear Reader, sometimes God calms the storm that rages around us and sometimes He just calms us. Trust in Him; He is your Refuge (Ps. 62:8), and He is the God of all comfort (2 Cor. 1:3).

LESSON 13

Have Faith

This lesson is tough because sometimes things just seem impossible. My grandfather's death stretched my faith to its limit. I remember driving home from the funeral and telling Lionel that I did not know whether or not I had enough faith to believe both that Peewee, my grandfather, was in heaven and that we would one day have a child. However, through the struggles with fertility and through the losses of loved ones, God has strengthened my faith.

God has often reminded me of the father in Mark 9. An evil spirit possesses his son and takes away his speech. The father brings his son to Jesus' disciples, but they cannot drive out the spirit. He then asks Jesus to do anything if He can. Jesus answers, "Everything is possible to the one who believes." The father then responds, "I do believe! Help my unbelief" (Mark 9:17–24). So many times I have felt like this father; and I have prayed his words, "I do believe! Help my unbelief." God has been gracious; He has given me the faith I needed for each day, and little by little He has increased my faith.

The author of Hebrews writes what we commonly refer to as the roll call of faith. He begins Chapter 11 with these words, "Now faith is the reality of what is hoped for, the proof of what is not seen. For our ancestors won God's approval by it" (Heb. 11:1–2). Then he lists both men and women who demonstrated their faith in God. This chapter encourages me when I see the struggles that people before me faced, how they believed and did not lose faith, and how God answered. I encourage you to take time to read this chapter that discusses Abel, Enoch, Noah, Abraham, Sarah, Isaac, Jacob, Joseph, Moses, Rahab, and others. They, too, faced trials that stretched their faith to its limits; but God did not fail. They trusted Him and He did more that they could imagine.

Regarding faith Jesus tells to His disciples, "If you have faith the size of a mustard seed… you can say to this mulberry tree, 'Be uprooted and planted in the sea,' and it will obey you" (Luke 17:6). I do not know if you have ever seen a mustard sea, but it is tiny! Yet, Jesus says that if we have even a tiny bit of faith, the impossible, what we could never imagine, becomes possible.

"Faith is the reality of what is hoped for" (Heb. 11:1). For what do you hope? Do you hope for God? Do you delight yourself in Him? "Faith is… the proof of what is not seen" (Heb. 11:1). We do not see God with our physical eyes, and we often do not grasp the bigger picture that He has in mind. However, we can be certain that His plan is to prosper us and not to harm us, to give us a hope and a future (Jer. 29:11). I know what I hope for—God. I also trust what I do not see—God.

My Dear Reader, God is able to do more than we could ever ask or imagine (Eph. 3:20–21); He is able to accomplish the impossible. Have faith in Him!

LESSON 14

God Heals Our Hurts

My heart broke at my grandfather's death because he was a tremendously special man to me. I cried and wept and cried some more. I prayed and cried, and in time God healed my hurt. Yes, the healing process took time, several months for that matter, but eventually the hurt did ease up. And before you ask, yes, I still miss my grandfather and I have cried on occasion (especially when I go see his grave), but the constant ache is gone.

I wish I could remember a good passage of Scripture to go with this lesson, but none come readily to mind; at least I cannot think of a verse that specifically says, "God heals our hurts." I can, however, think of many passages in Matthew where Jesus heals a physical infirmity: a man with leprosy (Matt. 8:1–4), a paralyzed servant of a centurion (Matt. 8:5–13), Peter's mother-in-law (Matt. 8:14–17), two demon-possessed men (Matt. 8:28–34), a paralytic (Matt. 9:1–8), a woman who had been bleeding for twelve years (Matt. 9:20–22), two blind men (Matt. 9:27–31), a mute man possessed by an evil spirit (Matt. 9:32–34), the daughter of a Canaanite woman (Matt. 15:21–28), a boy with a demon (Matt. 17:14–23), and two more blind men (Matt. 20:29–34). These stories and more appear in the other gospels: Mark, Luke, and John. I cannot help but think that if God can and did heal these physical problems, He can and does heal our hurting hearts. He is the Great Physician after all.

Peter writes, "Now the God of all grace, who called you to His eternal glory in Christ Jesus, will personally restore, establish, strengthen, and support you after you have suffered a little while" (1 Peter 5:10). My Dear Reader, take your hurts to the Lord. Tell Him how your heart aches, and let Him "restore, establish, strengthen, and support" you. Let Him heal your hurts.

LESSON 15

Stuffing Away Emotions

I spent the week after my grandfather's death dealing with my grief. I cried and I prayed, and I cried and prayed some more. I knew from past experience that I could not just ignore my feelings with the hope they would eventually disappear. When I stuff my emotions away, they tend to intensify and come pouring out all at one time.

Emotions are a part of life, a part of being human. You are going to be "up" some days and you are going to be "down" at other times. You will experience joy and you will suffer heartache. You cannot escape these or hide from your feelings. Sadly, when we try to stuff away our emotions, they build up inside of us until the dam holding them bursts. This usually happens at inappropriate times and in exaggerated ways in addition, the ones we love the most are often hurt by our outbursts.

Please do not get me wrong. I am not suggesting that you go around crying all the time or telling everyone you meet all the trouble that you are having. Exercise self-control; this is part of the fruit of the Spirit (Gal. 5:22–23). Your closest friends may need to know your struggles so that they can help you and so that they can pray for you. However, use discernment in choosing with whom you share your feelings and your problems.

Rather than holding in your emotions or blurting them out to everyone you meet, find constructive ways to deal with what you are feeling. First, pray to God and pour out your heart to Him (Ps. 62:8).

I promise He is big enough to handle your hurt or your anger (even if it is directed towards Him). Second, read the Bible, especially the Psalms. The psalmists were very open and direct about their feelings, and the psalms can be comforting and encouraging. Third, cry if needed; tears are a great emotional release and an excellent stress relief. Fourth, get the rest you need. Do not just stay up all hours of the night reading, watching TV, or playing on the computer. When faced with troubled times, sleep is often difficult for us, but do your best to get sufficient rest each night; then you will be better able to deal with your emotions. Fifth, talk to a trusted friend; sometimes just talking to someone helps us feel better. If necessary, seek help from a professional Christian counselor. Finally, look for ways to serve others. This helps you get your mind off your own troubles as you realize that everyone has struggles and that some problems are bigger than yours. Amazingly, God has taken some of my greatest hurts and turned the time of healing into some of my greatest times of service (not that I was great but what God did and how He worked through me was great). As God healed my hurts, He gave me a deeper capacity to love; He also opened doors for me that I might not have walked through otherwise.

My Dear Reader, do not just leave your emotions hanging out there. Let God help you sort through them; let Him heal you through time and through service.

LESSON 16

Enjoy the Memories

L ionel and I have enjoyed a couple of vacations to Walt Disney
World in Orlando, Florida. We greatly needed these vacations
at the time because they came after stressful months for us. Our
trips were truly "magical" as Disney advertises. We relish the memories
of these trips because of the carefree time we had and the closeness we
developed. Even now, on stressful days we often ask each other, "Can
we go to Disney tomorrow?" While we plan to return to Disney one
day, we are not planning to do so at the moment we ask the question.
The memory of our trip helps us smile, deal with the stress, and move
on. It reminds us that the problem will not last forever and that good
times will return.

Enjoy the good memories that you have. I am not suggesting that
you live in the past, but instead think about the fun times you have
shared with loved ones. Laugh over inside jokes. Celebrate life. Do not
hide the memories in the back of your mind; treasure them. They can
bring comfort as you rejoice over moments shared. I believe that God
gives us those memories to strengthen us through troubled times and
to help us heal after life's hurts and disappointments.

Shortly after my grandfather's death, my mother planned a special
evening to remember him. She cooked his favorite dishes, and she had
a special gift for me—a memorial tear necklace. The shape symbolizes
the tears shed over a death, and the rose engraved on it represents love.
The necklace summed up my feelings after Peewee's death. The rose on

it was even more special because it reminded me of the beautiful roses that my granddad had grown in the past. This necklace is a treasured and often worn gift, and it has become one of my favorite necklaces because of the memories it represents—cherished memories which have brought me comfort numerous times.

I cannot move away from a lesson on memories without somehow tying it to Scripture. I was wondering what verses in the Bible referenced memories, and God brought the Israelites to mind. They spent around four hundred years in slavery in Egypt. Then God brought them out of slavery into His Promised Land. On the night of their deliverance, God gave the Israelites very specific instructions, including what to eat and how to eat it. This became the Passover that was observed each year; it was a celebration of the victory that God had won, a festival of the freedom that He had given the Israelites, and a remembrance of the good that He had done (Ex. 11–13). Later after forty years of wandering in the desert, the Israelites had another great thing to remember: crossing the Jordan River and walking into the Promised Land. God kept the Jordan River from flowing so that the Israelites could cross the river (at flood stage, by the way) on dry land. When they had finished crossing, God told them to choose one man from each of the twelve tribes to carry a stone from the middle of the Jordan. The stones were to help the people remember what God had done and how they had crossed the river on dry land. They were a memorial about which children would ask and that their parents could use as an opportunity to tell what God had done (Josh. 3–4).

My Dear Reader, while you do not need to live always looking backwards, you should cherish your good memories. Write them down if you need to and enjoy them. Celebrate what God has done for you!

LESSON 17

Bad Memories

As I write this, Lionel and I have experienced our first failed fertility treatment. This is a huge disappointment and a memory that I had rather forget. A friend from work told me today that my faith must be a lot greater than hers because she was angry. She wondered why a good couple like Lionel and me had not had a baby. My words to her were something along these lines, "I have the same questions that you have. However, there have been things that happened in the past that I didn't understand at the time, and I have seen the good that God brought out of them. So I'm trusting God to bring good out of this and to do what is best." I choose not to focus on how bad some memories are; instead, I remember how good God is. As I struggle, I recall Lesson 5 from earlier in this book—God always knows and does what is best, even if I do not understand. God has been faithful through previous trials in my life so I trust Him through this fire, as well.

Like mine, not all of your memories are good. Please do not live looking backwards, regretting the bad that has happened. The past is the past and there is nothing that we can do to change that. However, since God does work all things for the good of those who love and obey Him (Rom. 8:28), there is good that He brings out of the bad circumstances. Focus on the good that He has done. Celebrate the victory He has given you. Cherish the lessons that He has taught you; write them down if you need to. One of the reasons I wrote this book is so that I do not forget the lessons that God has taught me over the last few years. There is a second reason that I wrote this book: God carried us through each difficulty, and I want Him to receive praise and glory. You, too, can praise God for the strength and comfort that He has given you in the past, for the good He has done, and for the lessons that He has taught you.

In the previous lesson, I mentioned the Israelites and a couple of the memories that they celebrated—how God worked good and delivered them out of slavery. Another Scripture related to memories occurs in the New Testament. The gospels record the death of Jesus. He was ridiculed and convicted in a mockery of a trial. He was beaten and was sentenced to die an excruciating death on a cross. However, God used Jesus' suffering to redeem us. God won the victory over sin, death, and the devil when Jesus died on the cross and then rose from the dead on the third day. We take the Lord's Supper to commemorate all of this. Paul writes about the Lord's Supper, "For I received from the Lord what I also passed on to you: On the night when He was betrayed, the Lord Jesus took bread, gave thanks, broke it, and said, 'This is My body, which is for you. Do this in remembrance of Me.' In the same way, after supper He also took the cup and said, 'This cup is the new covenant established by My blood. Do this, as often as you drink it, in remembrance of Me.' For as often as you eat this bread and drink the cup, you proclaim the Lord's death until He comes" (1 Cor. 11:23–26).

My Dear Reader, bad memories are a part of life, but God works everything out for the best. Do not focus on how bad your problems were; instead, think about how great God is. Remember the lessons that God has taught you out of the hard times, and definitely do not forget the good that He accomplished!

LESSON 18

Ask for Help

On the campus where I teach, I am one of four advisors of Phi Theta Kappa, the international honor society for community colleges. Serving as Phi Theta Kappa advisor is definitely a joy, but it is a lot of work. As one of our projects we decided to host a week long emphasis on health; the emphasis was entitled "Fit 4 ICC: Health Is in My Crosshairs." Health week turned out to be not so healthy for me. I ended up chairing this project along with one of our students, and I got too involved in it without asking for help.

Asking for help is hard for me. I am an only child; and while I had friends growing up, I learned to do a lot of things by myself. This independence carried over to adulthood as I learned to handle bills, groceries, car problems, etc. by myself. I also have a tendency to be prideful. I want to be able to say, "Look what I did!" with an emphasis on "I." The end result is that many times I take on too much and I do not ask for help when I need it. Health week was one of those instances; and by the time I realized I had overcommitted myself, I was too entrenched in the week to let go of the tasks that had to be accomplished.

My Dear Reader, God gives us family, friends, and others for support and for help. Sometimes we just need a cheerleader, someone to encourage us; at other times we need the physical assistance of someone. On occasion we need both inspiration and aid. If you are struggling, do not hesitate to ask for help and/or support. Now, I am not talking about going around with your hand out constantly. Do what you can; but when you reach the extent of your ability, ask for assistance. (Actually, make sure you ask for help before you get to the end of your rope and have to hang on to it for dear life!) There is nothing wrong with admitting that you have limitations and that you need help; remember that is part of why God has given us each other.

Galatians calls us to bear each other's burdens, "Carry one another's burdens; in this way you will fulfill the law of Christ. For if anyone considers himself to be something when he is nothing, he deceives himself" (Gal. 6:2–3). These verses sum up this lesson for me. I should do my part but my focus should not be on myself. I should ask for help when I need it, and in turn I should be willing to give help when needs arise. I should not think I am really "something", or in today's lingo "all that", when without Christ I am nothing and I can do nothing (John 15:5).

King Solomon, one of the wisest men ever to have lived, penned the following words: "Two are better than one because they have a good reward for their efforts. For if either falls, his companion can lift him up; but pity the one who falls without another to lift him up. Also if two lie down together, they can keep warm; but how can one person alone keep warm? And if someone overpowers one person, two can resist him. A cord of three strands is not easily broken" (Eccl. 4:9–12). God has given you family, friends, and others to help you and to support you so do not stubbornly try to do things just on your own. Ask for help when you need it.

LESSON 19

Open Eyes

Through several devotionals and experiences, God has shown me that my eyes must be open to opportunities to speak of Him and all that He has done for me, but I must confess that I have often been too caught up in myself to see the chances that God gives me. As I am writing today, God is convicting me of this. I remember the joy that I feel when I see and seize an opportunity to speak of God, and I recall the amazement I experience at how often those doors open as I begin to make the most of first one opportunity and then another. I want that again.

The book of Matthew records a parable that Jesus tells His disciples during His last week on earth. A man going on a journey leaves talents (a type of money) with each of three servants. Two of the three servants invest the money and gain more. The master praises them as good and faithful servants; and since they had been trustworthy with a little, he puts them in charge of more. The master invites the faithful servants to share his happiness. However, he calls the third servant wicked, lazy, and worthless because the third servant had just buried the master's money in the ground; he failed to invest it in any way. The master takes the money from that servant and throws him out (Matt. 25:14–30). I want to be like the faithful servants—looking for where God is working and eager to be a part. I do not desire to be like the third servant—a worthless servant, too wrapped up in myself to notice the paths that God wants me to follow.

My Dear Reader, God calls us to be faithful servants, to have our eyes open, and to avoid squandering opportunities that He gives us. In fact, before Jesus ascends into heaven after His resurrection, He speaks the following words to His disciples: "Go, therefore, and make disciples of all nations, baptizing them in the name of the Father and of the Son and of the Holy Spirit, teaching them to observe everything I have commanded you. And remember, I am with you always, to the end of the age... But you will receive power when the Holy Spirit has come on you, and you will be My witnesses in Jerusalem, in all Judea and Samaria, and to the ends of the earth" (Matt. 28:19–20; Acts 1:8). These words encourage us to tell others about God's precious gift of salvation; to teach others about God, His love, and His ways; and to be witnesses for Him wherever we go. However, to do any of these, our eyes must be opened to see the opportunities that God gives us.

Lord, open our eyes that we may see. Remove our blinders and help us see beyond ourselves. Let us see the opportunities around us each day to speak of You, and give us courage to walk through each door that You open for us. Help us to understand the urgency in making disciples. At the end of our lives, we want you to say, "Well done, good and faithful servants" (Matt. 25:21).

LESSON 20

Opportunities

While dealing with infertility caused much stress, God brought joy into my life through a student that I mentored. This relationship developed because of a God-centered conversation that was overheard. About the same time as this conversation, the Baptist Student Union on campus had been studying mentorship; and my soon-to-be mentee had been a part of this study. She had been praying for a mentor; and when she overheard my conversation, she realized that God had led her to me. I was thrilled! This was a privilege for me because I want God to be honored through my life and she had noticed God in me. My mentee and I began meeting once a week at lunch and our time together was such a blessing. Through this relationship God also brought into my life two other young ladies, and the four of us often studied the Bible together. All of this developed because of one conversation, one open door that God gave me and through which I walked.

Making the most of every opportunity is a lesson that God drives home to me time and time again. I usually ask God each day to open my eyes to opportunities to speak of Him and to help me make the most of each of those opportunities. Sadly, though, I am often too busy to even notice these opportunities. But when I am sensitive to chances to speak of God, He always blesses me. Each door that opens amazes me, and knowing that God chooses to use me humbles me.

Paul writes in Ephesians, "Pay careful attention, then to how you walk—not as unwise people but as wise—making the most of the time, because the days are evil" (Eph. 5:15–16). These words, while intended for the early church, are definitely true for us today! Time is running out because for every day that passes we are one day nearer either to our deaths or to the return of Christ. For Christians death is the beginning of life in heaven with God. However, for the lost death is the beginning of eternal separation from God; it is the beginning of eternal punishment in hell. For Christians the return of Christ is a joyous occasion because Jesus will take us to heaven with Him. For the lost all hope ends at the return of Christ for they will be eternally doomed to a place where there is much weeping and gnashing of the teeth (Matt. 8:12); they will be eternally doomed to the lake of fire (Rev. 20:15).

My Dear Reader, hell is just as real as heaven. We do not like to talk about hell and many people, including Christians, do not want to believe that hell exists; but it is real. Feel the urgency. We have a mission from God to tell the world about His salvation. Are you being careful how you live? Are you living as wise and not as unwise? Are you looking for opportunities to speak of God, and are you making the most of each opportunity?

LESSON 21

A Willing Vessel

Making the most of each opportunity (see previous lesson) and being a willing vessel go hand in hand. Being a willing vessel means agreeing to do whatever God asks you to do whenever He asks you to do it. It means walking in faith through the doors that God opens. God gave me the opportunity to mentor my student because I was a willing vessel. I was eager to make the most of opportunities that I saw, and I was ready for God to use me however and whenever. I was available to do whatever God asked me to do and He blessed my willingness.

Maybe you feel that you are not capable of doing what God has asked you to do. I cannot tell you how inadequate I felt to be a mentor. My walk with God and my life were far from perfect, but I knew that God would guide me and help me. Likewise, you do not need to worry about being capable; God will give you the ability to do whatever He asks of you. In fact, God can often better use us when we think that we are not capable than when we think that we are. When we consider ourselves inadequate, we rely on Him rather than on ourselves.

Several passages in the New Testament assure us of God's help. Hebrews 13:21 states that God will "equip you with all that is good to do His will, working in us what is pleasing in His sight, through Jesus Christ." Paul says in 2 Corinthians 9:8, "God is able to make every grace overflow to you, so that in every way, always having everything you need, you may excel in every good work." Paul also writes that God meets all of our needs (Phil. 4:19), and he tells Timothy that Scripture prepares us for good works (2 Tim. 3:16–17). Notice that each of these verses states that God gives us all that we need to do what He asks us to do. God is not going to leave you hanging; if He asks you to do something, He is going to be right beside you, helping you every step of the way. You may be surprised by the opportunities that God gives you and the impact that you have if you are obedient to Him and if you rely on Him.

All God needs is someone who is willing; then He can do much more than we could ever dream (Eph. 3:20). My Dear Reader, are you a willing vessel? Are you going to step out in faith and do whatever God asks you to do whenever He asks you to do it? If so, you will be blessed beyond measure!

LESSON 22

A Higher Standard

As a mentor to my student, I was held to a higher standard. This challenged me to walk each day with Christ—to pray continually, to study the Bible since I did not want to lead my student astray, and to live by God's ways. The questions she asked tested me so I dug deeper into God's word to find the answers to those questions and/or to support what I told her. This was a period of much growth for me as my mentee helped to hold me accountable.

James writes, "Not many should become teachers, my brothers, knowing that we will receive a stricter judgment" (James 3:1). This applies to teachers, mentors, and everyone in positions of leadership. For example, in my classroom I am held to a higher standard. I have to know more mathematics than my students so that I can better teach them and help them understand why we solve problems the way that we do. I have to make sure that I am not making careless mistakes; otherwise, I will confuse my students. I also have to be compassionate, willing to listen, and ready to answer questions. Sometimes I have to correct my students when they are wrong, and sometimes they have to correct me when I make a mistake. I am responsible for doing my best to help the students in my classroom learn. The same is true in the spiritual realm.

First, teachers, mentors, and leaders need to know God's Word backwards and forwards. They must allow God to write it on their hearts so that their actions and words are not contrary to what He commands. They must seek God's guidance in what they teach so that their lessons are timely and appropriate. They must submit to the leadership of the Holy Spirit and be sensitive to what to say, when to say it, and how to say it. They cannot compromise God's values and they cannot compromise God's Word. If they do either of these, they will face consequences such as losing their joy in serving or even losing their leadership position.

Teachers, mentors, and leaders not only teach God's Word verbally, but they also teach God's ways by how they live. Since they often lead by example, they should not just "talk the talk" but they should also "walk the walk." In other words, they should not say one thing and then do another; their words and actions should match. They must live purely and with integrity.

Finally, teachers, mentors, and leaders are responsible for the people that God entrusts to their care. They are accountable for lovingly and boldly speaking God's truths. They are answerable for gently correcting those entrusted to their care so that their "students" learn to obey God and to walk with Him.

My Dear Reader, if God has called you to teach, to mentor, and/or to lead, make sure that you cling tightly to Him and that you live by His Word. Remember that you are held to a higher standard.

LESSON 23

Spiritual Warfare

God opened my eyes to the spiritual battle that is around us each day. Through books and Bible studies I developed an awareness of how Satan fights against God and tries to keep us from Him. The more I studied, the greater my sensitivity to spiritual warfare became, and I began praying through the spiritual armor (belt of truth, breastplate of righteousness, feet fit with readiness from the gospel, shield of faith, helmet of salvation, and sword of the Spirit) in the mornings as I got ready for work so that I would be better prepared for the battles I would face each day (Eph. 6:10–18). God impressed the reality of spiritual warfare on my heart so strongly that it became a topic that I often talked about with the young ladies that I mentored.

You may think that I have totally lost my mind discussing spiritual warfare, but I tell you that it is real! There are many Scriptures that refer to it. 2 Samuel describes David's experience with a battle beyond what his physical eyes could see. While he is fighting the Philistines, God tells him to attack the enemy from a certain line of trees. He warns David to wait until he hears the sound of marching in the tops of the trees because that meant that He (God) had gone out in front of David to attack the Philistines (2 Sam. 5:23–24). 2 Kings 6 refers to another unseen army. Aram is at war with Israel, and the king of Aram is hunting down Elisha because he (Elisha) keeps spoiling his (the king's) plans. When the king finds Elisha in the city of Dothan, he (the king) surrounds the city. Elisha's servant goes out early in the morning, discovers the horses and chariots of Aram all around the city, and panics; but Elisha encourages his servant to not be afraid because the enemy is outnumbered. Elisha then prays, asking God to open his servant's eyes. When God answers Elisha's prayer, the servant sees that the hills around them are full of horses and chariots of fire (2 Kings 6:8–23). The book of Daniel records another spiritual battle. An angel appears to Daniel, but he had been slow in coming to Daniel because a battle with the devil had detained him until Michael, another angel, came to help him (Dan. 10:12–13). The book of Jude also mentions a battle between Michael and the devil in which Michael disputes with the devil over the body of Moses (Jude 9). Finally, the book of Revelation describes the battle between God and Satan that will take place at the end of time.

The letters of Paul include other references to spiritual warfare. To the Corinthians Paul writes that even though we live in the world, we fight differently; we do not fight with worldly weapons but with spiritual ones, weapons that are powerful because of God (2 Cor. 10:3–4). To the Ephesians Paul explains how we need spiritual armor to fight Satan (Eph. 6:10–18). He warns, "Put on the full armor of God so that you can stand against the tactics of the Devil… This is why you must take up the full armor of God, so that you may be able to resist in the evil day, and having prepared everything, to take your stand" (Eph. 6:11,13).

Notice that Ephesians 6:11 emphasizes why we are to put on God's armor: "so that you can stand against the tactics of the devil." The devil is a crafty fellow. Jesus calls Satan a liar and the father of lies, and He says that no truth can be found in Satan (John 8:44). He refers to Satan as a thief who came to steal, to kill, and to destroy (John 10:10). Peter further warns that the devil is like a lion seeking out its prey (1 Peter 5:8). My Dear Reader, Satan is a liar and a schemer, and his tactics are purposed to destroy your life. I do not say this to make you afraid; after all, we have no need to fear because Jesus won the victory over Satan! I say this to warn you. You need to be aware of the devil's tactics so that you can resist him.

Now, notice the wording in Ephesians 6:13. Paul does not say that we needed to resist *if* a day of evil comes; he urges us to resist *when* the evil day comes. I believe that day is already here. Too many people have believed Satan's lies and have turned to sex, money, drugs, popularity, success, etc. to satisfy them when only Christ can do that. God's values have been compromised and our nation is in a moral crisis. Society in general now openly accepts actions that previous generations considered immoral. Just look at prime time television; we have gone from *The Cosby Show* with good, clean values to programs that accept casual sex and that promote the homosexual lifestyle. God calls His children to fight for His ways and to stand firm for Him. To do this, we must put on His armor.

Too many people are ignorant of the spiritual warfare that is going on around us; the battle is for souls, and eternal destiny (heaven or hell—eternal life with God or eternal punishment apart from God) is at stake. An ignorance of this war is what Satan wants because if we do not know or do not think about the battle then we are not fighting against him. If we are unaware of the spiritual battle and the tactics that the devil uses, then he has a hold on our lives. The stronger the hold of the enemy in our lives, the more ineffective we are in telling others what Jesus has done for us and the fewer people we impact for God's kingdom.

My Dear Reader, just because you do not see the battle does not mean that it is not there. Do not be fooled by Satan's tactics and his lies! Stay grounded in God and His Word; both are unchanging truth! Put on your spiritual armor, stand firm, and fight for the Lord!

LESSON 24

The Fight Against Satan

Ephesians 6:12 states, "For our battle is not against flesh and blood, but against the rulers, against the authorities, against the world powers of this darkness, against the spiritual forces of evil in the heavens." We do not fight against people; we fight against Satan and his minions. This seems to be a lesson that comes back to me again and again. How often do I get angry and try to fight against people?

One fall God emphasized this lesson to me. I mentioned in the previous lesson that I had begun praying through the spiritual armor every day, and one day the verse above stuck out to me. After I had spent extra time helping a particular student, I suspected her of cheating on a test. As a teacher, you can imagine how much this angered me; and I held it against her. Through this verse God reminded me that I was not fighting against my student. Yes, I needed to take actions to prevent cheating (hers and that of others), but the real battle was one that I could not see. Yes, I needed to be cautious and watch for further cheating, but I had no right to remain angry with this student. What was done was done and I needed to move on. I needed to forgive her and remember that my battle was not with her; my enemy was (and is) the devil.

After God reminded me of this, my attitude toward this student changed. When she enrolled again in one of my classes about a year and a half later, I had to remember this same lesson. I do not fight against my students; yes, I need to do what is right, but my battle is not with people; I am fighting with God against the devil. The devil is our enemy—not people!

LESSON 25

Called to Pray

As if struggling with infertility was not burden enough, I also lost contact with a special friend during this time. The circumstances leading up to this loss of contact and the subsequent lack of communication had me extremely concerned. Many times this friend came to mind and many times I prayed. I did not know all of the problems, the emotions, and the "goings-on" of that individual, but I did know that God called me to pray—over and over, again and again. In time, God answered my requests.

When God calls you to pray, there is always a reason. You may not fully comprehend the situation, but God does. He knows and is concerned about the needs and wants of every person on our planet, and one way that He invites us to join His work is through our prayers. So when God brings someone to mind, pray; then pray again, and pray some more until He gives you peace.

James writes, "Is anyone among you suffering? He should pray. Is anyone cheerful? He should sing praises. Is anyone among you sick? He should call for the elders of the church, and they should pray over him after anointing him with olive oil in the name of the Lord. The prayer of faith will save the sick person, and the Lord will restore him to health; if he has committed sins, he will be forgiven. Therefore, confess you sins to one another and pray for one another, so that you may be healed. The urgent request of a righteous person is very powerful in its effect" (James 5:13–16). This passage emphasizes that we are to pray for each other through sufferings, through sicknesses, and through joys; therefore, be sensitive to the Spirit's leading in your prayers. When God lays someone on your heart and mind, pray for that person. You may never know the struggles he or she is facing, but you can be assured that the effects of your prayers will be "very powerful."

My Dear Reader, do not get so distracted that you miss hearing the Spirit. Do not be so busy that you forget to pray. Instead, listen to God; then pray when and how He leads. God promises to hear and to answer our requests.

LESSON 26

Two or Three Sides to Every Story

I am ashamed to say that too many times in my life I have jumped to conclusions without having all of the information. I have listened to bits and pieces of "evidence" from a third party and made assumptions without talking to the source. I have made inferences when I heard only one side of the story, and sadly many times the deductions to which I came were wrong. I remembered this when I lost contact with the friend that I mentioned in the previous lesson.

Sometimes situations are as they seem to be, but too many times we jump to conclusions based on only one side of the story. When we do not have all of the facts, we often make assumptions that are not true. Proverbs 18:8 says, "A gossip's words are like choice food that goes down to one's innermost being." The same warning appears in Proverbs 26:22. Listening to only one side of a story and not having all the facts is similar to listening to gossip. When we jump to conclusions based on the story we heard, we let the "choice food… [go] down to" our hearts, and doing so is a mistake.

A friend once reminded me that there are usually three sides to every story: his side, her side, and the truth. I have found this to be true. As humans, we tend to want people to agree with us so we stretch the truth and make our side of the story seem bigger or worse than what it really is. We also tend to leave out our part or contribution to the situation as we tell the story, and in turn we emphasize the other person's faults. We do these things to gain sympathy in our pain and to gain support in our disagreements.

My Dear Reader, please realize that there is always more than one side to every story. Whether the story is yours or that of someone else, there is another side. If possible, listen to all sides of the story. Even if you (or someone you love deeply) have been hurt, you (or the one you love) are not the only person involved and probably not the only one hurt.

Proverbs 19:2 states, "Even zeal is not good without knowledge, and the one who acts hastily sins." Do not be hasty and jump to conclusions without knowledge. Wait and listen. Hear all sides of the story before you make assumptions.

LESSON 27

Divorce

D ivorce is never pretty. I already knew this, but I experienced it firsthand on my journey of faith as I watched the divorces of several of my friends unfold. For those getting the divorces, there is usually much hurt which needs healing, much anger through which to sort, and much bitterness of which to let go. Children get caught in the middle and are often asked to choose between their mother and their father. They have their own wounds which demand healing, their own anger which requires soothing, and their own bitterness which strains for release. Family and friends take sides, often without knowing the whole story. All involved must learn to forgive and to let go of any anger over the situation. After a divorce everyone (the ones getting the divorce, the children, extended family, and friends) must adjust to a new normal, and change is not easy for any of us.

My Dear Reader, divorce is not God's plan. In Mark 10 the Pharisees question Jesus about divorce, asking Him if it is lawful. He answers them by asking what Moses had commanded. They then state that Moses permitted divorce. Jesus responds, "He wrote this command for you because of the hardness of your hearts. But from the beginning of creation God made them male and female. For this reason a man will leave his father and mother [and be joined to his wife], and the two will become one flesh. So they are no longer two, but one flesh. Therefore, what God has joined together, man must not separate" (Mark 10:5–9).

I am not criticizing those who have gotten divorces; I know and love many good people who have divorced for one reason or another. However, one of the reasons I believe that divorce is not God's will is God knows the hurt that accompanies divorce and He wants to spare us that hurt. (On a side note, I once heard a sermon about the times that God allows divorce: adultery, addiction, abuse, and abandonment.)

My Dear Reader, if you are thinking about divorce, please think again. Pray, and genuinely seek God's direction and His hand in reconciliation with your spouse. Also, if you know of anyone who is recovering from a divorce, pray for them. Be available to listen and to offer encouragement.

LESSON 28

The Valleys of Questions and Waiting

As Lionel and I struggled with infertility, each month that I did not conceive was devastating. I remember shedding tears nearly every month because I was upset that I was not pregnant. We had prayed and prayed; we had believed that God would give us a child. However, I did not get pregnant and this saddened us. Every month added to the tears that we had already shed, and our longing for a child and our hurt continued to increase. Nevertheless, God was with us and He was teaching us. We chose to turn to Him in our disappointment and our hurt.

During this time, I often poured out my heart to God asking Him why we struggled with infertility, questioning how much longer we would have to wait, pondering what we were doing wrong, wondering if my emotions were normal, and feeling alone. Maybe you are in the same boat—hurting, disappointed, questioning, frustrated, and/or lonely.

If you feel that you are all alone in your struggles, I guarantee that you are not alone! First and foremost, God promises to never leave you or forsake you (Deut. 31:6, 8). Second, there are others who have faced what you are facing and who have survived. They have struggled with the same emotions that you feel and they have overcome. You are not alone! You have a God Who loves you beyond measure, and there are people who are willing to come alongside you and help you through your difficulty.

Are you questioning whether or not your emotions are normal? They probably are. Disappointment and hurt are part of the consequences that we suffer because of Adam and Eve's sin. We live in a fallen world and life will not be perfect this side of heaven. We will have ups and we will have downs. Sometimes the roller coaster will be such a wild ride that we struggle to find balance; but through the joys and the sorrows, pour out your heart to God. Tell Him your emotions; He is big enough to handle them and you can trust Him.

When you have not received an answer to your prayers, do you wonder, like I did, what you are doing wrong? My Dear Reader, if you are praying and believing and living by God's Word, you are not doing anything wrong; in fact, you are doing just what you should. Even if you are not seeing the answers to your prayers and your struggles, do not give up and do not lose faith. Cling to God; hold tightly to Him. Keep pouring out your heart to Him and laying your requests before Him. He will answer in His time and in His way, both of which are perfect.

Maybe you are wondering why you are facing the struggle you are in now or why the wait is so long. God may not give you the answer to those questions. Lionel and I faced months of fertility tests and treatments, and we still do not have a child. I do not understand why God has not yet chosen to bless us with a child. We have been walking in obedience to Him. We have believed and prayed and not given up, but God has not yet answered our prayer for a child. However, I trust that His timing is best, that His plans are for our good, and that He wants to give us hope and a future (Jer. 29:11).

Is waiting on God easy? Not by a long shot. The road that Lionel and I have faced has not been easy; it has been long and hard and full of roller coaster emotions. However, God has been with us every step of the way, and I know that He will continue to be with us. Why has God not yet answered our prayers for a child? Why has the wait been so long and still continues? I do not know but I do choose to trust Him. And you, too, can trust God through your questions and your waiting. He will never fail!

LESSON 29

The Story of Job

The book of Job is the story of a man who faces devastating losses. In one day he loses his oxen, his donkeys, his sheep, his camels, his servants, and his children. Another day Job loses his health as Satan afflicts him with painful sores from head to toe. His wife criticizes him and suggests that he turn away from God. When Job's friends see him after the losses he endures, they almost do not recognize him. For seven days none of them talk because they see how great Job's pain is. However, when his friends do speak, they add insult to injury by accusing him of sin.

Despite all of these losses and difficulties, Job choses to trust God rather than turn away from Him. After Job loses his livelihood and his children, his response is as follows: "Naked I came from my mother's womb, and naked I will leave this life. The Lord gives, and the Lord takes away. Praise the name of Yahweh" (Job 1:21). Job replies to his wife's criticism, "You speak as a foolish woman speaks… Should we accept only good from God and not adversity?" (Job 2:10). In speaking with his friends, Job says about God, "Even if He kills me, I will hope in Him" (Job 13:15). He further states, "But I know my living Redeemer, and He will stand on the dust at last. Even after my skin has been destroyed, yet I will see God in my flesh. I will see Him myself; my eyes will look at Him, and not as a stranger. My heart longs within me" (Job 19:25–27). Job does not understand why his life is suddenly wrought with troubles, but he does believe that God is faithful.

For what must have seemed like a long time to Job, God is silent in the midst of Job's suffering. When He does answer Job, He never explains why Job suffers; He only gives examples of His power and His sovereignty (Job 38–41). After hearing God speak, Job humbly replies, "I know that You can do anything and no plan of Yours can be thwarted. You asked, 'Who is this who conceals My counsel with ignorance?' Surely I spoke of things I did not understand, things too wonderful for me to know. You said, 'Listen now, and I will speak. When I question you, you will inform Me.' I had heard rumors about You, but now my eyes have seen You. Therefore I take back my words and repent in dust and ashes" (Job 42:2–6).

I wonder how many times I, like Job, have spoken ignorantly before God, how many times I have forgotten that God can do all things, how many times I have talked of things that I did not understand, how many times I have overlooked the fact that no plan of God's can be thwarted, and how many times I have spoken of things too wonderful for me to know. I know the answer: way too often. As I write, I remember all of the questions that I have asked God as we struggled with infertility. My questions were similar in nature to Job's; and like Job and his friends, my understanding has been lacking. Too often I have darkened God's counsel with words that were ignorant (Job 38:2); I have tried arguing with God and pleading for my own way. However, God has been gracious to me and He has been patient with me.

In the dialogue recorded in the book of Job, God never does explain to Job why he lost so much, and He may never tell you why you are struggling and hurting. Sometimes God allows problems in our lives to make us better. Sometimes God permits troubles to discipline us (Heb. 12:3–11). Sometimes God lets trials come to draw us closer to Him. Sometimes God allows hurts so that we can later comfort others (2 Cor. 1:4). Sometimes God permits suffering in our lives and we never know the reason. Our place is not to question His reasoning; we do not see the big picture that God sees. Our place is to trust Him and to rest in His promises.

My Dear Reader, there is hope. God does prosper Job again; in fact, He doubles what Job had before. God blesses Job more in the last part of his life (after his losses) than He had blessed Job in the first part of his life (before his suffering). He even gives Job seven more sons and three more daughters, and Job lives to see four generations of children (Job 42:10–17). God can do the same for you. You may not experience the same blessings that Job did, but He will deliver you through (not necessarily from) the problems. As Joel prophesies, God will redeem the years the "locusts" of problems ate (Joel 2:25).

LESSON 30

Will I Trust God?

Just as God speaks to Job in his suffering (Job 38–41), God also spoke directly to my heart on three separate occasions. He asked me three very distinct questions while we waited for a child.

"Will you trust Me?" was the first question that God asked me. This question surfaced many times during my journey of faith, and it appeared in several different forms. Will I trust God with the conception of our child? Will I trust God with the timing of our child? Will I trust that God's ways are best even if I do not understand them? Will I trust God during the wait though the wait is long? Will I trust God through the hurt? Will I trust God with any possible complications?

Will I trust God with the timing of our child, and will I trust Him during the wait? Yes. Remember Lesson 10—God's timing is perfect. I do not understand the wait but I trust His perfect timing. The amazing thing is that God has a special plan for our child and this plan includes when our child will be born. Our child being born too soon would not fit into God's plan to use him or her. Our child will be born at just the right time to grow up and be used by God in just the right way.

Will I trust God with any complications or even possibly a miscarriage? When we first decided to have a child, I was extremely concerned about miscarrying. How would I handle being pregnant and losing a child? I was scared but God reassured me. Through a friend He reminded me that in His hands everything would be okay—whether that meant a miscarriage or complications. So I came back to the question God asked me, "Will you trust Me?" Will I trust God with any possible complications? Yes, He is sovereign over all and He is the Great Physician. Am I concerned about difficulties during pregnancy? Yes, I am; however, I know that God will heal and that He will deliver us through the problems. Am I apprehensive about miscarrying? Yes, I still do not know how I would handle it. However, I know that if I do miscarry, God will be with us in that and He will comfort us.

Will I trust God through the hurt and disappointment? Most definitely! Past experience has taught me that God is faithful even when I do not understand His ways. Remember Lesson 5—God always knows and does what is best. Lesson 12 reminded us that God is the God of all comfort and that He comforts us when we hurt. And Lesson 14 stated that God heals our hurts. So I will trust God even if I hurt and even if I face disappointment.

Will I trust that God's ways are best? Yes! He has proven time and time again that He knows what He is doing. Situations always turn out so much better when I give Him control than when I try to handle them myself. Do I understand God's ways? Not always but I trust that He has a plan and a purpose for us and for our child.

Will I trust God with the conception of our child? This is a question that I have to come back to many times. I begin to worry. What if I do not conceive? What if the fertility treatments do not work? What if…? Honestly I still struggle with this question. The other questions I can answer immediately, "Yes!" but this one is harder.

The Bible is full of couples who struggled with infertility. Abraham and Sarah wait twenty-five years for a child. In the meantime they try to take matters into their own hands when they get tired of waiting. (See the story of Hagar and Ishmael found in Genesis 16.) At the proper time, though, God fulfills His promise to Abraham; and he and Sarah have a son named Isaac (Gen. 12,21). Isaac and Rebekah wait and pray for a child, and again at the proper time God gives them Jacob and Esau (Gen. 25:20–26). Jacob's wife Rachel is barren for years while her sister has child after child, but eventually God blesses Rachel with two sons (Gen. 29:31–30:24; 35:16–18). Hannah is barren and she fervently prays for a child. God answers her prayer with Samuel, and then later

God blesses her with three other sons and two daughters (1 Sam. 1–2). Zechariah and Elizabeth do not have children, but an angel appears to Zechariah and tells them of the son they would have. John the Baptist is their child (Luke 1). Was the waiting easy for any of these couples? I am sure it was not. Did they struggle with faith and with emotions? The Bible records both.

Will I trust God with the conception of our child? Yes, I will. I will trust God because I come back to the answers to the other trust questions. I will trust God because His timing is perfect. I will trust Him because His ways are best. I will trust Him because He is the Great Physician. I desperately want a biological child but I trust God. If His answer is no, then He has another child in mind for us, maybe one already born, maybe one yet to be conceived, or maybe He will satisfy our desire for a child in some other way that we could never imagine.

God asked me, "Will you trust Me?" My answer is yes. Now I ask you. Will you trust God? I do not know what problem(s) you are facing. Maybe you, too, are struggling with infertility. Maybe you are grieving the loss of a loved one. Maybe you are concerned about health problems or financial issues. Maybe you just have a lot of "What if…" questions. Will you trust God? Proverbs 3:5 – 6 says, "Trust in the Lord with all your heart and do not rely on your own understanding; think about Him in all your ways, and He will guide you on the right paths." My Dear Reader, trusting God is not always easy but it is always best!

LESSON 31

Is God Enough?

The second question that God asked me was "Am I enough?" Every month Lionel and I hoped that I would be pregnant, but disappointment followed this anticipation. Some months the frustration and longing were worse than others. One day I was standing at the kitchen sink trying to deal with my distress. I was crying and pouring out my heart to God, telling Him how much I hurt and how desperately we wanted a child. In the midst of my hurt, my tears, and my prayers, God spoke to my heart gently but clearly, "Am I enough?" I paused for a moment and I answered God's question, "Yes, Lord, You are enough."

In the midst of my hurt and my desires, I had lost focus and had forgotten that God truly is enough. Do I still want a child? Most definitely! But I also realize that even if God chooses not to give us a child, He is enough. Only He can truly satisfy. A child will bring joy, but a child can never take the place of God; a child can never completely satisfy.

What do you desire most? Family? Friends? A child? A husband? A job? A car? Clothes? Shoes? Money? None of these are bad in and of themselves; they are all good things, and most of them are necessary. However, these will never fulfill you. They will always leave you longing for something more or wanting something else. God created us with a God-shaped hole, a vacuum that we all try to fill but that can only be satisfied by Him. Isaiah writes, "Come, everyone who is thirsty, come to the waters; and you without money, come, buy, and eat! Come, buy wine and milk without money and without cost! Why do you spend money on what is not food and your wages on what does not satisfy? Listen carefully to Me, and eat what is good, and you will enjoy the choicest of foods" (Isa. 55:1–2). This is God's invitation to those who are longing. Do not seek things to gratify you; they will only disappoint. Seek God, and you will find great delight and fulfillment.

One of my favorite psalms is Psalm 103, and it describes how God satisfies us. Here the psalmist writes, "My soul, praise the Lord, and do not forget all His benefits. He forgives all your sin; He heals all your diseases. He redeems your life from the Pit; He crowns you with faithful love and compassion. He satisfies you with goodness; your youth is renewed like the eagle" (Ps. 103:2–5). My Dear Reader, what could be better than this? God forgives us. God heals us. God redeems us. God gives us love and shows us compassion. God satisfies us.

What is your greatest desire? For what are you longing? Turn that desire over to God. He will satisfy you with good things (Ps. 145:16). Pray with the psalmist, "Satisfy us in the morning with Your faithful love, so that we may shout for joy and be glad all our days" (Ps. 90:14).

LESSON 32

Will I Walk Away from God?

The third question that God asked me on my journey of faith was "Do you want to leave Me too?"

The day that God asked me this question, I was again upset, disappointed, angry, and confused. You name the emotions, and I probably felt them because we had been praying and praying for a child but still remained childless. I was talking to God and telling Him my hurt and my disappointment. I asked Him, "Why? Why haven't you given us a child? We have prayed and prayed. We have waited. We have trusted. Why do we still not have a child?" God's answer was the question that He asked me, "Do you want to leave Me too?"

When God asked me this question, He brought to mind a story from John 6. In this story Jesus teaches the people and tells them that He is the Bread of life. However, many of those who are listening find His words too hard to swallow so they decide not to follow Him. Jesus asks the twelve disciples if they want to leave Him too. Peter answers, "Lord, who will we go to? You have the words of eternal life. We have come to believe and know that You are the Holy One of God!" (John 6:68–69).

My answer to God's question was immediate and was the same as Peter's, "Lord, to whom else would I go? Only you have the words of life. I believe and know that you are God." Through this simple question God helped me regain perspective.

My Dear Reader, do not leave God even if you do not understand the hurt that He allows in your life. To whom else would you go? Money can be lost in an instant. Homes, clothes, cars, and other possessions can burn in a fire or be destroyed by a hurricane, a tornado, or a flood. The buzz of alcohol or other drugs is temporary. Fame is short-lived. Success will only last until something new and better comes along. Sex is meaningless outside of God's parameters of marriage between one man and one woman. Your health will eventually decline. People will fail; even those who love you most and whom you love most will one day disappoint you. To whom else would you go? Only God never fails. Only God is always be faithful. Only God keeps every one of His promises. Only God is always working for your good. Only God can completely satisfy you. Only God can give you life. Only God can offer you eternal life with Him. Say with the psalmist, "Who do I have in heaven but You? And I desire nothing on earth but You. My flesh and my heart may fail, but God is the strength of my heart, my portion forever" (Ps. 73:25–26).

LESSON 33

Extending Grace and Love

As a teacher, I have opportunities every day to extend grace and love through my responses to my students. Am I harsh with them, or do I take time to listen? Do I react to my students with indifference, or do I show them love? Do I truly care about their grades, or am I more concerned about my evaluation? All of these are important and challenging questions for me to answer. After all, God has called me to be an ambassador for Christ (see Lesson 8), and one way I can do this is to show grace and love in my classroom. (Please do not get me wrong; this does not mean that I fail to hold my students accountable. Each of my students must maintain certain grades to pass, and I expect them to be honest in their work. Extending grace and love to my students is not giving them better grades than they earn or excusing bad behavior, but it does affect my attitude toward my students and my communications with them.)

While God gives me multiple chances to show His grace and love in my classroom, He has also given me other grace "adventures" to teach me. Some involved simple mistakes and miscommunications that were easily resolved. Others produced awkward situations that presented a potential for grudge-holding and that kept me awake at night pondering my response. In each situation God inevitably reminded me of how He had treated me and told me to do likewise—to be hospitable, to love, and to forgive. As I did these (with His help!), God healed broken relationships, brought together those who had been apart, and built friendships.

Grace is receiving the good things that you do not deserve. God has been so good to us. He forgives our sins. He gives us eternal life, an opportunity to live with Him forever. He blesses us with joy, peace, and hope. In fact, He pours His riches into our lives, and we do not deserve any of what He has done for us. Our calling and our response to His grace is simple: to extend grace to others, even when they do not deserve it. How do we do this? We do not excuse or condone bad behavior, but we love the person despite that behavior. We let go of bitterness and let God bring healing and reconciliation. We show kindness to others, we give generously yet wisely, and we offer a helping hand to someone in need. We listen. We forgive. Paul writes to Timothy that he should be strong in God's grace (2 Tim. 2:1) because when we are strong in grace, then we are reflecting God to the world around us.

God calls us not only to extend grace, but He also commands us to love. Why? Very simply: because He first loved us (1 John 4:11,19). We do not deserve God's love but He loves us anyways. God is holy and perfect, and we are not (Rom. 3:23); we all fall short of God's expectations. In other words, we sin; we do what we want to do rather than what God wants us to do. "But God proves His own love for us in that while we were still sinners, Christ died for us" (Rom. 5:8). Did you catch that? God loved us so much that He gave up His Son for us (John 3:16). Now, that is love!

We, in turn, should love as God loves us. In fact in the book of John, Jesus tells His disciples that He is giving them a new command: to love each other just as He loves them (John 13:34). He says that people will recognize His disciples because of their love (John 13:35). Jesus' command still applies to us today; we are to love others just as God loves us. This means that we love unconditionally. We love generously and sacrificially. We love no matter what. We speak words of love, and we demonstrate our love through service to others. Because of love we put others' needs and wants before our own while still physically taking care of ourselves (getting the rest we need, eating right, exercising, etc.). Love enables us to look out for the good of others even if this entails saying "no." Love marks us as belonging to God, and our love reflects God's love to the world.

Maybe you are thinking, "But So-and-So doesn't deserve grace and love so why should I extend either to him/her?" My Dear Reader, we did not deserve God's grace or love, but He gave us both. Do you remember 2 Corinthians 5:20 about being God's ambassador (see Lesson 8)? The next verse states that Jesus took our sin so that we could be holy like Him (2 Cor. 5:21). Any righteousness in you is not because of the good that you do; it is because of Christ's work in you. In Him and in Him alone you become the righteousness of God. We have no right to judge others because we, too, sin. We miss the mark and do not measure up to God's standards. Some people's sins are more visible than that of others, but that does not mean that the ones with less visible sin are any better.

Extending grace and love to others is usually not an easy thing to do. In fact, it is often quite difficult but this is what God calls us to do. He tells us to show others grace and love just as He demonstrated both to us.

Reacting in Anger

W hen Lionel and I first decided that we needed to talk to my doctor about beginning fertility tests, I was a basket case! In fact, the whole week before my first appointment I was very much on edge. I had no idea what to expect, and the unknown was nerve-wracking for me. On the day before my appointment, I received some news at work that completely upset my apple cart. This information should have been a small adjustment for me, but instead I reacted to the news with vehement anger. I remember the emotions vividly. My upcoming appointment caused me stress, and my job had added yet another stress. Ugh! I was furious and I let everyone know how angry I was. I might have had a good reason to be upset; however, I am ashamed to say that I let my temper get the best of me. Instead of adjusting and letting the situation roll off my back (like water rolls off the back of a duck), I overacted; and God reminded me that I should not let anger win.

Ephesians 4:26 states, "Be angry and do not sin. Don't let the sun go down on your anger." This chapter continues by encouraging us to remove anger from our lives so that we do not give Satan any opportunities to discredit or distract us (Eph. 4:27, 31). Notice that these verses do not say that we should never be angry; anger is a natural emotion. However, these verses tell us not to let our anger cause us to sin. As Christians (and God's ambassadors), anger should not be our overriding emotion or the emotion that prompts our decisions. We should not be the fool mentioned in Proverbs 29:11 who "gives full vent to his anger", but rather we should be the wise man who "holds [his anger] in check." Oh, how I wish I had heeded these words in my situation at work! Yes, maybe being angry over my situation was reasonable, but everyone with whom I came in contact did not need to hear about it. I would have been wise to keep myself under control that day. My Dear Reader, maybe you, too, have a good reason to be angry; but do not let your anger cause you to sin. Slow down. Take a deep breath. Count to 10 or 20 (or even higher) if needed. But whatever you do, do not react in your anger and thus do something that you may later regret. Rather than blowing up or giving "full vent to" your anger (like I did), find constructive ways to deal with it. Consider talking to God, talking to a trusted friend, or exercising. Since self-control and patience are fruit of the Spirit (Gal. 5:22–23), control your anger with His help; think and pray before you react.

As God was prompting me to control my anger, He also reminded me of how my anger affects the people around me. Proverbs 15:1 tell us that speaking gently soothes anger but speaking harshly enflames anger. Proverbs 22:24 cautions us about becoming friends with someone who gets angry easily. Proverbs 29:22 continues these warnings, "An angry man stirs up conflict, and a hot-tempered man increases rebellion." These verses prompt me to think about how my words and attitudes affect others. Ouch! How many times have my angry words stirred up someone else's anger? How many times have I been the "friend" who is easily angered? The answer is too many times. Our words are powerful. When we discuss the actions of someone who hurt us, then others may become angry that someone caused us distress. Or our description of a situation that makes us angry may remind others of circumstances that made them angry. Either way, our anger stirs up the anger of someone else. Yes, sometimes you need to talk with a trusted friend, but all too often we "vent" to people when we should have spoken to God first. Ask God for help, for patience, for direction, and for self-control. Pour out your heart to Him, and let His peace that is beyond our understanding flood your heart (Phil. 4:7).

God's peace is not the only thing that can help us deal with our anger; His love also affects whether or not we become angry easily. 1 Corinthians 13 describes the characteristics of love; among the qualities listed in this chapter are patience and the ability to not easily be angered (1 Cor. 13:4, 5). We all will become angry at some point; it is a natural emotion, but we need to let love rule and not anger. When we bask in God's love and allow it to overflow into our lives and out of our lives, we begin to love as He loves. Then little by little love produces more patience and less anger.

James writes, "My dearly loved brothers, understand this: Everyone must be quick to hear, slow to speak, and slow to anger" (James 1:19). Oh, how this verse pricked my heart when I read it! I was definitely not slow to become angry in my situation at work, and I was also not slow to speak; everyone who would listen knew how angry I was. However, God is gracious; He has forgiven my anger, and He continues to work in me to make me more patient, more loving, and less easily angered. My Dear Reader, let God work in you. Ask Him to forgive you for your anger and to help you become "quick to hear, slow to speak, and slow to anger."

LESSON 35

Witnesses

One summer Lionel's dad Buford faced open heart surgery due to the blockage of several of the arteries in his heart. Since the surgery was such a big risk, we could not let him face that risk without knowing his eternal destiny. Lionel and I assumed that Buford had made a choice to follow Jesus, but we had never talked to him about it. Before Buford's surgery Lionel discussed Jesus, salvation, and heaven with his dad; Buford reassured us that he was a Christian. (My Dear Reader, if you are unsure about what salvation means or what your eternal destiny is, then turn to the last lesson in this book. You will read information about the most important decision you will ever make.)

Salvation is a priceless treasure—a treasure that we are not to keep to ourselves but to share with others. As Christians God calls us to be Jesus' witness (to share the treasure of salvation) wherever we go (Acts 1:8). This means that we need to live out our faith in all that we do, but it also means that we need to talk about our faith. We should not just be silent Christians sitting on the sidelines. God calls us to actively witness; and He gives us the Holy Spirit to guide us, to show us when and to whom to speak, to teach us what to say, and to empower us to tell others about our Heavenly Father (John 16:5–15; Acts 1:8).

While God calls us to witness, this can be a frightful thing. You may have questions, like I do, such as: What if someone makes fun of me? What if someone rejects me? What if someone classifies me as a radical? God addresses these questions in His Word. What if someone makes fun of you? As Christians, we can expect to be ridiculed for our faith. In the book of John Jesus says that if people persecuted Him, they would also persecute those who follow Him; if people hate Him, they will also hate His followers (John 15:18,20). He further states that we belong to Him and not to the world (people who do not follow Christ); because He chose us and we bear His name, the world hates us (John 15:19,21). Too many times, I think that we American Christians have become too comfortable with where we are and all that we have, and we do not want to rock the boat. We are afraid to face a little "persecution", but what we encounter is minor compared to the persecution that many Christians experience around the world: loss of job and/or property, excommunication from their families and social groups, torture, prison, and even death. The early church, too, was confronted with much persecution. They were unfairly tried and put in jail (Acts 5,12). They were killed (Acts 7). They were beaten; they were stoned (2 Cor. 11). And what was their response? They rejoiced because they were considered worthy of suffering for Christ, and they continued to proclaim the gospel (Acts 5:41–42). Wherever the persecution scattered them, they preached about Jesus (Acts 8:1,4). What if someone makes fun of you? It does not matter. God does not call us to fit in with the world; we do not belong to it. God calls us to be different. If people ridicule you for your faith, then rejoice that you are considered worthy of suffering for Christ, and continue to be a witness wherever you go. What if someone rejects you when you tell him about Jesus? He is not really rejecting you so much as rejecting Jesus (John 15:18–25;16:2–3). If God tells you to speak to someone and you are obedient, the result is not in your hands; you have done what God told you to do. The result is between God and that person. What if someone calls you a radical? Be glad that they recognized that there is something different about you. Accept the fact that we are just passing through this world. We are aliens and strangers here on earth (1 Peter 2:11); our true citizenship is in heaven (Phil. 3:20).

My Dear Reader, I write this lesson not only to you, but I also speak to myself. All too often I do not witness to others about God's love. I get too wrapped up in my own little world, my own busyness, or my own pain that I fail to see a world that needs Christ. I am often too selfish to hear God's call to speak to someone, or I am afraid to speak up. I have the same questions and fears you do. However, God reminds me of these words that Paul writes to Timothy, "For God has not given us a spirit of fearfulness, but one of power, love, and sound judgment" (2 Tim. 1:7). We do not have to fear witnessing to others about Jesus because God is with us; His Spirit lives in us and will teach, encourage, and strengthen us (John 14:15–18,26).

Do not pass up a chance to witness to others about Jesus and His ultimate gift; we never know how much time that we have left (James 4:13–14). We may have tomorrow but we may never see tomorrow come. Only God knows when our lives will end and/or when the world as we know it will be destroyed (2 Pet. 3:1–13). The person to whom you are talking may die before the end of today, and this could be his last opportunity to hear about God's love. On the other hand, your life could soon end or Jesus could return (1 Thess. 4:13–18), and you may never again have occasion to share what Jesus has done for you.

There is an urgency for us share God's salvation. People who are lost, people who are searching but do not know where to turn, and people who will spend eternity in hell if we do not tell them about God surround us. We are God's plan for spreading the gospel, and there is no plan B. We are accountable to God (Rom. 14:12; Heb. 4:13). If God urges you to share the gospel with someone, be obedient; be faithful. Be a witness.

LESSON 36

Love One Another

I know that I have already written about extending love and grace, but let's explore these topics again. I told you that sometimes God reinforced the lessons that He taught me, and this is a lesson that kept coming up. We will focus on love in this lesson; then in the next lesson we will look at grace again.

While Buford was in the hospital following his open heart surgery, I had the pleasure of spending time with him, and I developed a special relationship with my father-in-law. I would read while Buford slept, but I also enjoyed the time that we spent visiting. We would talk about all kinds of topics: coffee, what I had for lunch, the outbuilding that Lionel and I were converting into an office, groceries, advertisements in the newspaper, his hometown, etc. Through these times that we were together, God deepened my love for Buford; and I am thankful for the relationship and the closeness that we developed. I no longer loved Buford just because he was Lionel's dad; I loved him because God had given me precious time with him.

The love that God gave me for Buford amazes me. As I mentioned, before his surgery I loved him because he was Lionel's dad; but as I spent time in the hospital with him, I quickly loved him for who he was and not just because he was family. The growth and depth of this love could come from only one source—God. My love for Buford changed after just one day with him, and I do not usually love someone that quickly.

I praise God for His work in me and for the love that He gave me for my father-in-law.

This was not the first time that God has given me love for people. Each semester He helps love my students, no matter who they are and even in spite of the difficulties some of them cause me. My second year of teaching stands out in my mind. Before the school year started, I asked God to help me love my students; and when my students walked into the classroom the first day, I loved them. I had not even met them and I loved them! A love like this could only come from God.

My Dear Reader, Jesus calls us to love one another. In the book of John He says, "I give you a new command: Love one another. Just as I have loved you, you must also love one another. By this all people will know that you are My disciples, if you have love for one another" (John 13:34– 35). Jesus tells us to love others as He has loved us so think for a minute about how He has loved us. Jesus' love is a sacrificial love; He lay down His life for us! His love is unconditional. We do not deserve His love but He offers it to us anyway. His love is selfless. He is God's Son, but He did not flaunt that fact; He was a humble servant who gave His life willingly (Phil. 2:6–11). We are to have the same kind of love for others: a selfless, unconditional, sacrificial love. This does not necessarily mean that we die for others, but this kind of love puts others' needs and wants before our own whether or not the other person is deserving of that love. If we love others in this way, then we will be reflecting Christ to a world that so desperately needs Him.

Some people are not hard to love; they are humble, kind, appreciative, and good-natured. Others, however, are more difficult to love because of their actions, because of their attitudes, and/or because of their responses to you and your love. If you are having trouble loving someone, then ask God to help. Ask Him to give you love for people. Then let His Spirit work in you to develop His fruit: LOVE, joy, peace, patience, kindness, goodness, faithfulness, gentleness, and self-control (Gal. 5:22–23).

LESSON 37

Extend Grace

God reminded me about extending grace to others as Lionel and I began caring for his dad, first through his hospital stay and then through nearly five months of illness. Following Buford's heart surgery I spent many days at the hospital with him, and Lionel came by after work each day to see his dad. While Buford was in rehab, we visited him; and when he returned to the hospital (for the last two and a half months of his life), we continued to check on him. We became his caregivers, not only taking care of him (going with him to doctor's appointments and buying things that he needed) but also managing all of his financial business. This period of our lives was stressful, and the few months we cared for Buford were long. However, God called us to show grace and that was what we did.

As we showed grace to Buford, God blessed us. A day that particularly stands out in my mind was the day before the doctors released Buford from his first hospital stay. I had gone to the rehabilitation facility to fill out the paper work for Buford's admission, and then I headed to the hospital. On my way to the hospital I was sad and discouraged, realizing the weight of signing papers for someone else's healthcare. However, when I walked into Buford's room at the hospital, he smiled at me with a grin that filled his whole face and said, "Hey, Girl!" That made my day, and I realized the blessing in extending grace.

My Dear Reader, God has shown grace to you. He forgives your sins (1 John 1:9). He comforts you (2 Cor. 1:3–4). He gives you peace that passes understanding (Phil. 4:7). He heals you (James 5:15). He meets all of your needs (Phil. 4:19). He blesses you beyond measure. He does for you more than you could ever ask or imagine (Eph. 3:20). Anything good in your life is because of God's grace. If God has shown so much grace to you, shouldn't you extend grace to others?

LESSON 38

Forgive

Along my journey of faith as God taught me (through many different situations) to extend grace to others, He also showed me that I needed to forgive. Ephesians 4:32 says, "And be kind and compassionate to one another, forgiving one another, just as God also forgave you in Christ." Did you catch that? We are to forgive others just as God has forgiven us. Yikes! I know God has forgiven me much; this means that I, in turn, should forgive others the wrongs that they do to me.

In the book of Matthew when Jesus is teaching His disciples about forgiveness, Peter asks Him how many times he should forgive the same person. Should he forgive seven times? By the teachings of the religious leaders at the time, forgiving seven times would have been extremely gracious. However, Jesus answers Peter that he should forgive seventy-seven times (or seventy times seven times, depending on which translation you read). Then He tells a parable about two servants. One owed his master ten thousand talents, a sum of money that he could never repay; we'll call this first servant John. The other servant (we'll call him Billy) owed his fellow servant John one hundred denarii, a relatively small sum of money especially compared to what John owed. The master came to collect the money that John owed him, but John begged for mercy and the master forgave the debt. John then demanded that Billy repay him. However, when Billy begged for mercy, John had him thrown in prison rather than forgiving the debt (like the master had forgiven his own debt). When the master was informed of John's actions, he pointed out the wrong that John had done; John should have shown mercy to Billy, just as the master had shown to him. The master threw John in prison until he could repay the debt (Matt. 18:21–34). We are like John. We have a debt that we could never repay; we sin (do wrong, go against God's wishes), and there is a penalty for that sin—death, eternal separation from God, hell. The master is Jesus. He forgave our debt when He died on the cross; He paid our penalty. He has removed our sins from us. In fact, Psalm 103:12 tells us that the distance He has taken our sins from us is the same as the distance between the east and the west. That's a long way! And Micah 7:19 says that our sins have been hurled into the sea, never again to be dredged up. Now, we have a choice when "Billy" hurts us: we can forgive as we have been forgiven or we can hold onto a grudge. Jesus closes the parable with a warning, "So My heavenly Father will also do to you [put you in prison like the master had John jailed at the end of the parable] if each of you does not forgive his brother from his heart" (Matt. 18:35). If we choose not to forgive, we will be in a prison of our own making—a prison of bitterness, a prison of anger, a prison of misery, and a prison of sin because we did not obey God.

I have two warnings about forgiveness. One, I wish I could say that forgiving means completely forgetting, but as humans we often do not forget. For us, forgiveness is letting the past stay in the past and not bringing it up again and again and again; it is letting go of the hurt and the anger. Two, forgiving also does not necessarily lead to reconciliation. Both people have to be willing to lay aside differences, and sometimes the other person is not willing. Also in some situations (such as abuse) we do not need to be reconciled; for our own protection the relationship does not need to be restored.

My Dear Reader, God has forgiven you of all of your sins; you also need to forgive the people who have hurt or wronged you in any way. Let go of the anger and bitterness, and let God heal your hurt.

LESSON 39

Better To Give Than To Receive

"It is more blessed to give than to receive." These are words of Jesus that Paul quotes in Acts 20:35, and I have experienced the truth of these words in many ways. First, as we cared for Lionel's dad, I cannot tell you how often he would smile at me when I entered his room or how many times he would say "Hey, Girl!" enthusiastically when he saw me. His smile and his words encouraged me. Second, I like physical touch; I am a hugger. Buford, however, did not always express love that way so I was thrilled when he would hold my hand or when he would reach out for a hug. Third, many times in the past God blessed me when I gave financially. I never lacked what I needed even when I sacrificially contributed to His causes. God amazed me by stretching my money to the end of the month, by providing a raise to cover the costs of what He wanted me to give, and by making the gas in my car last longer than usual when I needed it to do so.

When we give to others, when we serve as God leads, He blesses us. He gives us strength to do what He asks us to do. He gives us joy, satisfaction, and fulfillment as we use our talents and abilities. We have peace because we know we are obeying God. He allows us to see how He is working, and seeing the results of His work is exciting! Words cannot begin to describe all of the blessings that God gives us; however, I can assure you that if you are serving and giving as God leads, He will bless you!

I do have one word of caution for you before we leave this lesson. Do not agree to everything! Just because someone asks you to give or to serve does not mean that you should. Pray before committing to a gift or to an act of service. Yes, God will bless you when you serve and when you give, but only if you are serving and giving as He leads. If you step out of His will, you will find yourself run down, frazzled, uncomfortable, and unfulfilled. My Dear Reader, pray and then serve and/or give as God leads.

LESSON 40

God Answers Prayers

I know that I have already mentioned this lesson. In fact, "Answered Prayers" was the first lesson of this book; but as I have told you before, God repeated some lessons along my journey. God's answering my prayers was one of these recurring lessons. I have seen firsthand the power of prayer, and this power amazes me.

While I cannot go into details, there was a particular time on my journey when Lionel and I sensed the urgency of prayer for us and for our friend whom I will call Karen. We asked some close friends from church to pray with us over the situation, and then we went into our bedroom and spent 1 to 2 hours in prayer and in deep discussion. I cannot begin to tell you how fervently we prayed. We prayed for direction for us in handling the circumstance, and we prayed for Karen—for a change of heart for her, for her to let go of bitterness, for comfort for her, and for her to make wise decisions despite her current emotions.

Lionel and I experienced the power of prayer that afternoon/evening. First, God gave us direction that we needed; He showed us what our role was in the situation. Second, God gave us strength to do what was right. I remember walking into the circumstance the next day and telling God that He would have to fight this battle for us, and He did! God gave us the strength, the reassurance, and the perseverance that we needed. Third, God changed Karen's heart. The person we saw the next day was very different from the one with whom we had been dealing. Only God could have so drastically changed her.

My Dear Reader, God hears and answers our prayers (Ps. 3:4); never doubt that fact. Whatever the need is (whether the need is yours or that of a family member or friend), pour out your heart to Him and trust Him with the answer. He is able to do much more than we could ever imagine (Eph. 3:20).

LESSON 41

Friendship

Buford's first follow-up appointment after his heart surgery happened to fall on the first morning of a new school year. I had planned to leave the house a little early to give us plenty of time to get to the doctor's office, especially since there was rain in the area. The morning was flowing smoothly until I arrived at the rehabilitation facility where Buford was staying. I do not remember everything that happened and I will not go into detail of what I do remember; however, the day turned sour and we were almost late for the appointment. We had further problems at the doctor's office so by the time I took Buford back to rehab and arrived at work, I was barely holding back the tears. Thankfully, I had friends to listen and to help me regain emotional control. These friends were a blessing that day; moreover, God has given us many friends for whom we are grateful. Our friends have prayed for us through Buford's health issues and through our own struggle with infertility; and we appreciate their support, their encouragement, their prayers, their shoulders on which to cry, and their listening ears.

My Dear Reader, you may never know the hurt that others feel and you may never fully understand their situations, but you can be a friend. You can just be there; the presence of a friend is comforting. You can listen when they need to talk, and yes, I did say listen and not talk because sometimes you really do not need to say anything. You can be a shoulder on which they can cry. So many times I just needed a shoulder on which to cry and a friend to give me a hug.

You can also cry with them as my friends often cried with me. You can pray for them. We would never have survived the last few years without the prayers of family and friends. Those prayers helped give us strength, wisdom, and encouragement to live through each day and each decision. You can send cards to encourage them and to let them know that you are thinking about them and praying for them. If you are not a "card-writer", then send an encouraging message through e-mail or through Facebook (the message should be a private message not a message written on the person's Facebook wall). I cannot tell you how encouraging Facebook messages were to us, especially through Buford's health problems; the support that others offered through these messages comforted us. You can call them and ask how they are doing. I can remember several occasions when someone called or e-mailed just to check on me; those small acts meant so much to me. You can give them genuine compliments. One of my students nearly every time she came to see me called me "Beautiful", and many days this would turn my day around for the better. Ask God how you can best be a friend, and then follow in obedience what He tells you to do.

Proverbs speaks much about friends. "A friends loves at all times, and a brother is born for a difficult time" (Prov. 17:17). "A man with many friends may be harmed [or depending on the translation: 'a man with many friends must be friendly'], but there is a friend who stays closer than a brother" (Prov. 18:24). "Don't abandon your friend or your father's friend, and don't go to your brother's house in your time of calamity; better a neighbor nearby than a brother far away" (Prov. 27:10). My Dear Reader, do not abandon your friends. Be a friend that loves at all times. Stick close to your friends just as Jesus sticks close to you.

LESSON 42

Being a Servant

Through several situations in taking care of Buford, I learned what being a servant truly means. For instance, Lionel and I arranged our schedules so that we could take his dad to doctors' appointments. We managed Buford's finances. We visited him often, and we made sure that he had the clothes and other items that he needed. Sometimes our tasks for Buford were tedious and menial, and at other times they were larger and overwhelming. Overall, the practice of serving was a humbling experience as we learned how to put Buford's needs before our own wants. We gave up a lot of time and energy in the last months of Buford's life, but what we gave up does not matter; what matters is that we were faithful to God's call to serve.

The book of Mark records the request of two disciples to be seated at Jesus' right and left sides in heaven (Mark 10:35–37). After this request Jesus speaks about servanthood, "You know that those who are regarded as rulers of the Gentiles dominate them, and their men of high positions exercise power over them. But it must not be like that among you. On the contrary, whoever wants to become great among you must be your servant, and whoever wants to be first among you must be a slave to all. For even the Son of Man did not come to be served, but to serve, and to give His life—a ransom for many" (Mark 10:42–45). In this passage Jesus calls us to service; He says that ones who are truly great are those who serve. While God has blessed some of us with leadership skills, we must not let the leadership roles go to our heads; instead, we need to follow Jesus' example and be servant leaders. Our purpose is to serve as Jesus served so that the world sees God's love in and through us. As servants we put the needs and wants of others before our own, stepping in to help when we see a need (but please do not forget to take care of yourself in the process—get the rest you need, exercise, eat healthy, etc.).

My Dear Reader, Jesus is the perfect example of a servant. He gave up His life for you! Whom is God calling you to serve, and how does He want you to serve them? Be obedient to God's call. Remember that giving is better than receiving (Acts 20:35).

LESSON 43

Difficult Decisions

As Lionel and I cared for Buford, life settled into a routine. We adjusted to being caregivers, and we learned to find a new balance. We gained power of attorney for Buford so that we could make decisions for him both financially and medically, and this was one of the best documents we could have had him sign. Admittedly the day that we took the documents for him to sign was a tough day, but we did need the power of attorney to take care of him. We did not want to take away anymore of his independence than necessary; however, these documents were extremely helpful for us in the months to come.

Discussing power of attorney (financial and medical), future health care, and end-of-life decisions (life support or no life support) is not easy. In fact, I have yet to have this discussion with my parents, but these issues need to be addressed. You need to know what your plans and your loved ones' plans are. Making these decisions sooner rather than later will be much easier. I speak from experience: emotions make decisions difficult and putting off these decisions until they are necessary increases the emotions involved and complicates the decision-making process.

My Dear Reader, I do not mean to be so blunt, but I really do not know of another way to put this lesson. At some point in time you may become a caregiver for a loved one, and you need to plan ahead for that time. To best care for your loved one, you need to know what he or she prefers. I firmly believe that God calls us to be good stewards (1 Cor. 4:1–2; 1 Peter 4:10), and part of being a good steward means addressing difficult issues and planning for the future.

LESSON 44

Just What You Need

Our original goal when Buford went to the rehabilitation facility was for his health to improve so that he could go back home and live on his own; but because of the complications he experienced, we had to develop an alternate plan. We began to realize that Buford may not ever be able to go back home so we began looking at nursing homes in the area and praying about which home would be best for Buford when the time came. Making these long-term care decisions for him was difficult. However, God guided us through that time, and He blessed us by sending us deer.

Now I know you may be wondering what I mean about God sending us deer. We have a patch of woods behind our house, and from time to time we have wild animals that wander into our yard: bunnies, foxes, and deer, in particular. God knows that I love bunnies; and often on a trying day, I see a bunny in the yard. Seeing that bunny brings a smile to my face and reminds me of God's sovereignty, His love, and His care. How else could a bunny hop into a yard just when I need to see it? (By the way, we do not usually see bunnies when life is smooth, just when the days are tough.) In the same way on the day that God sent us deer, Lionel and I had planned to visit our third and final nursing home, a process that was not easy for either of us. The nursing home was in our town so I met Lionel at our house after work. When we got ready to leave for the nursing home, we looked out the French doors in our bedroom and saw not a bunny but deer, and not just one deer—two fawns. God knew that we needed more than just a bunny that day so He sent us deer to remind us of His love, His care, and His sovereignty.

Psalm 10:17 says, "Lord, You have heard the desire of the humble; You will strengthen their hearts. You will listen carefully." My Dear Reader, isn't it great to know that God strengthens us? He points us to an encouraging Bible verse just when we need it. He sends a person with a compliment when we are discouraged. He touches us with a song when we are hurting. He sends us deer or bunnies on a trying day. We have a great God Who loves us tremendously, a great God Who reaches out to us when we are hurting and/or discouraged, and a great God Who is the Father of compassion and the God of all comfort (2 Cor. 1:3). When you are discouraged, when you are hurting, look to God; He is always there for you, and He will give you just what you need.

LESSON 45

God in the Small Things

My Dear Reader, God always knows what we need and He will always meet that need, but sometimes we must be willing to look for God in the small things. I mentioned in the previous lesson that God often sends Lionel and me a bunny on the tough days or sometimes He even sends a deer or two. Those are small things in which we have learned to look for God.

I can remember one morning that God brought me joy in another small thing. He sent me a squirrel to make me smile. Now you may be wondering, "What is so special about a squirrel? We have a yard full of them." We do, too, but this particular squirrel (I will call him Sparky for fun) was quite interesting to watch. The garage to our house is detached, and I can see the roof of the garage out of the window over our kitchen sink. As I was washing dishes, I became fascinated watching Sparky. He would pick up an acorn from the patio between the house and the garage, put the acorn in his mouth, climb the crepe myrtle tree, and then sit on the corner of the roof to eat his acorn. Then he would repeat the process. Climb down, pick up an acorn, climb the tree, and eat on the corner on the roof. Climb down, pick up an acorn, climb the tree, and eat on the corner on the roof. Sparky did this several times; and I laughed because I thought, "This poor squirrel is using more energy climbing up and down the tree from the roof to the ground than he is taking in!" After watching him for a minute or two, I pointed him out to Lionel who also became fascinated by Sparky. I know this may seem like such a little thing, but God used Sparky to bring a smile to both of our faces that morning. And God continues to use Sparky to make us smile when we remember his antics that day.

At a singles' retreat that I attended before Lionel and I were married, the speaker suggested finding something to remind us of God's love. He suggested flocks of birds because we see them often. Shortly after the retreat, a former student of mine passed away, killed in a car accident; and I went to the funeral home for visitation. I was nervous about going because I had never met her parents, but I wanted to give them my condolences and express to them what a joy she had been to teach. Upon leaving visitation I sat in my car and cried. Then when I pulled myself together, I began driving back to work to teach a night class. As I headed back to campus, I saw a flock of birds and was reminded of God's love. This was a little thing, but I was learning to look for God in those small things.

Another time a friend of my parents went missing for several days, and my parents were distraught. I was praying over the situation as I was walking one evening. I kept praying and praying and praying. Then I looked in the sky and there was a rainbow. At that moment God's peace flooded my life. Again this was a little thing, but God used the small thing to remind me of His love and to bring me peace.

My Dear Reader, God is able to do the great and the grand things (Eph. 3:20), but He does not always choose to work that way (1 Kings 19:9–18). Learn to look for Him in the little things: an animal that you love, a beautiful sunset, a rainbow, a rose, a… you fill in the blank. God is there and He is working. Learn to see His hand at work and His love reaching out to you.

LESSON 46

Praying for Direction

As Lionel and I cared for Lionel's dad while he was in rehab, we had to carefully make decisions. Some of these decisions were linked to Buford's care, and some were associated to our own lives. Whenever possible, we prayed over our decisions (both big and small), asking God to show us what the right action was. We needed wisdom from God; in fact, we could not have made the correct decisions without His help.

For example, a small decision I had to make was related to a planned trip. I serve as one of four advisors of the honor society on our campus, and every year in the fall we travel to a regional conference. The year of Buford's surgery the conference was to be held in New Orleans, Louisiana—about seven hours away from where we live. I was undecided about the trip; while Buford's health seemed to be improving, I did not want to be that far away from home if he were to have complications. I earnestly prayed and asked God what to do. Do I go on the trip or do I stay home? God gave me a peace about the trip so I went. I had a wonderful time, and Buford had no health problems while I was away. God blessed me when I prayed for direction, listened to His answer, and obeyed what He said.

The New Orleans trip was just one of the many decisions that Lionel and I had to make during this period of our lives. Many times we needed wisdom, and God reminded us of James' words, "Now if any of you lacks wisdom, he should ask God, who gives generously to all and without criticizing, and it will be given to him" (James 1:5). As humans our imperfections have tarnished our understanding. We see life through glasses tainted by sin, by hurt, by anger, and/or by own desires. We have a tendency to rationalize decisions so that we get or do what we want; however, the things that we desire are not necessarily best for us. Since our vision is clouded, we need God's wisdom. Only His wisdom is perfect and untarnished since He is holy. In fact, Paul describes God's wisdom in Romans 11:33, "Oh, the depths of the riches both of the wisdom and the knowledge of God! How unsearchable His judgments and untraceable His ways!" Yet God desires to teach us, to share His wisdom with us, and to guide us. All we have to do is ask. Then when we pour out our hearts to Him seeking help and wisdom, He listens and He generously and graciously answers. This is what James wrote.

My Dear Reader, if you need direction and/or if you are searching for what is the right action, then ask God. His wisdom is perfect and He will show you what to do. While walking in God's will is not always the easiest, I guarantee there is no better place to be.

LESSON 47

Take Care of Yourself

T ake care of yourself. This was probably the most important lesson that I learned while caring for Lionel's dad. Too many times I have tried to do too much; I overcommit myself, and I end up stressed and frazzled. In fact, I still struggle with this at times. I love to go and to do, and I want to be active and involved; however, I am learning that I cannot do everything. I have to set limits, and sometimes that means saying "no" to an activity so that I can rest and take care of myself.

After my trip to New Orleans with Phi Theta Kappa, Buford was admitted to the hospital. To make a long story short, the wire that held Buford's sternum together (after his open heart surgery) had pulled loose, and then this led to other complications. He spent from the end of September until the first part of December in the hospital, staying more in CCU (Critical Care Unit) than he did in a regular room. Lionel and I made many trips to the hospital to see his dad; and we also made a couple of trips to Buford's hometown to take care of his bills, mail, and other business. These months were trying months for all of us, and life was a careful balancing act. I learned to pray before committing to something, and I learned to say no and to realize my limitations rather than stretching myself thin.

In 1 Corinthians Paul writes that our bodies are the temple of the Holy Spirit, that we are not our own, that Jesus paid the price for us (see the last lesson in this book for more information about this), and that we need to honor God with our bodies (1 Cor. 6:19–20). While he is specifically referencing sexual immorality and our need to stay pure, I believe that these verses apply to taking care of ourselves as well. First, make sure that you eat right and get the nutrition you need; over time poor nutrition will greatly affect your health. Second, get the rest you need each night; do not stay up playing on the computer, watching television, or trying to catch up on tasks. You need rest and sleep to keep up your strength and to maintain your immune system. Third, exercise. Our bodies are made to move, not to be sedentary. Take time to exercise. You will feel much better, have more energy, and be less stressed if you do.

My Dear Reader, if you do not take care of yourself, you will not be able to serve as God calls you. So eat nutritiously, exercise, get the rest you need, and learn to say no when appropriate.

LESSON 48

Abortion

In the midst of Buford's health issues, I had a discussion with my gynecologist about fertility tests and treatments. We had tried Clomid, a drug which causes women to ovulate, but that was unsuccessful so my doctor scheduled an HSG (hysterosonogram). This test would check to see if my fallopian tubes were blocked, and it honestly ended up being one of the worst medical procedures I have experienced. After dealing with the physical discomfort during the test, I was bombarded with the emotional distress of unfavorable results. Long story short, the test showed that my tubes might be blocked which meant that I might not be able to have children.

This news devastated me. I cried and cried and cried some more. I hurt deeply and I was angry. How come unwed mothers get pregnant and I cannot? How come people who will have abortions get pregnant and I cannot? How come…? Why would God give us a desire to have a child just to have the desire dashed to the ground? I grieved for the child that I might never have.

I have always been pro-life but much more passionately after experiencing fertility problems. After the HSG I first wondered at the fairness of how someone who did not want a child could get pregnant and abort that child when at the same time people like Lionel and me could not have a child but desperately wanted one. I thought of the babies that are aborted each year, and my heart hurt. I grieved not only for the child I would not be able to have but for the children who do not even get a chance to live. Then I realized that if abortion hurts my heart so deeply, I could only imagine how much it hurts God's heart. You see, God is the Author of life. Psalm 139:13 says, "For it was You who created my inward parts; You knit me together in my mother's womb." In Jeremiah 1:5 God is talking to Jeremiah; and He states something similar, "I chose you before I formed you in the womb." God is the Creator and the Giver of life. He knits us together in the womb; and as the Psalmist writes, "[We] have been remarkably and wonderfully made" (Ps. 139:14). God gives us life, and His Word tells us that taking that life away is sin (Ex. 20:13).

My Dear Reader, despite what the media tries to tell you, life begins at conception when God starts knitting a baby together; and ending that life is wrong.

LESSON 49

Strength When We Need It

B ecause of the unfavorable results from the HSG, my doctor referred us to a fertility clinic. Lionel and I had a peace about going, but this did not mean that keeping that appointment was easy for either of us. When the day of our appointment came, Lionel and I both were nervous wrecks! I was shaking so badly that I had trouble filling out the paperwork at the doctor's office, and Lionel was in just as bad a shape. What would the doctor say? How much would everything cost since our insurance would not cover the fertility treatments? God gave us strength to "survive" the appointment, and I cannot say enough good things about our doctor at the clinic and about the clinic itself. Everyone was very kind and they helped to put us at ease. Our doctor was understanding and flexible since neither of us had fertility benefits with our insurance. In addition, he gave us hope. He said that the original HSG results were not reliable, and he suggested redoing the HSG along with undergoing a battery of other tests. We left that day with more hope than we had had in about a week, and we were grateful for the strength that God had given us.

Our appointment at the fertility clinic was on a Wednesday. On Friday (two days later) I received a phone call from the hospital that was caring for Buford. Though the call came during one of my classes, I knew I had to answer my phone because I recognized the hospital's number. One of Buford's doctors called to tell us that they could do nothing more for him and that we needed to consider hospice to make his last days as comfortable as possible. This news was shocking, discouraging, and disappointing because up to that point the conversations we had had with medical personnel had been positive. After that phone call I do not know how I was able to teach the rest of that class, to teach my next class, and to tutor students during my office hours; however, I realize that God gave me the strength that I needed to function throughout the rest of the day and to break the news to Lionel when he got home that evening.

The Bible refers much to the strength that God gives us. Philippians 4:13 says, "I am able to do all things through Him who strengthens me." The psalmists call God their strength and proclaim that God gives them strength (Ps. 18:1,32; 28:7; 46:1; 118:14). In a song recorded in Exodus, Moses and the Israelites praise God for being their Strength (Ex. 15:2). And Nehemiah tells us that God's joy is our strength (Neh. 8:10). Finally Isaiah 40:30 – 31 encourages us with these words, "Youths may faint and grow weary, and young men stumble and fall, but those who trust in the Lord will renew their strength; they will soar on wings like eagles; they will run and not grow weary; they will walk and not faint."

My Dear Reader, when you are tired and weary, when you are at the end of your rope, when you do not think you have the strength to go on, God is your strength!

LESSON 50

Life and Death

I mentioned in the previous lesson that Buford's doctors had told us to consider hospice for him. After this conversation, Lionel and I began looking at hospices in the area. We also instructed the hospital to take steps to prepare Buford for hospice: weaning him off the high flow CPAP (which helped him breathe but did not breathe for him), changing him from continuous feeding through his feeding tube to a limited number of "meals" each day, and removing his restraints. We wanted him to be as comfortable as possible through this process so we were cautious and prayerful in each decision that we made. However, when the hospital staff tried removing the CPAP, Buford struggled to breathe so they reconnected him to a ventilator to breathe for him. We realized at this point that we would have to make the end-of-life decisions that we had hoped we would never have to make.

Lionel and I agonized over the decision to remove Buford from the ventilator; in fact, this was probably the most difficult decision that we have ever made. We firmly believe that life is precious, and we did not want to take a life. However, after much prayer we decided that removing life support was the right decision, and then we left Buford's life in God's hands. The decision that we made was not a decision to kill Buford by taking him off the ventilator; it was a decision to lay his life in the hands of the Lord and to trust Him to do what is best. Psalm 116:15 says, "The death of His faithful ones is valuable in the Lord's sight." God knew the right time to bring Buford home to Him, and He guided us in the decisions we made leading up to that time.

Several days before he died, we asked Buford if he knew God as Savior; and he fervently shook his head yes. Then two days after the hospital staff removed him from the ventilator, Buford passed away; God took him home to heaven. The days leading up to Buford's death were tough, to say the least, but God gave us strength. He gave us guidance, and there was never a moment of that week that He was not in His control. And when Buford died, we knew he was in heaven with God and that he was whole once again. Never again would he have to suffer.

My Dear Reader, life is a gift from God. He is the Author of life, the Creator of life, and the Giver of life. He numbers our days. He knows when each person will be born and when each will die. From the day of our birth to the day of our death, our lives are in His hands; and there could be no more capable hands than His.

God has reminded me that life is a gift that we are meant to enjoy. Life can be quite a wild ride at times; but He has been teaching me to enjoy the moments that I have, to make the most of the opportunities before me, and to live life to the fullest. Now, this does not mean that I should step out of the boundaries and guidelines (laws, if you will) that God has put in place for my own protection; but I realize that life is short, that opportunities may not come again, and that there is joy in walking with God each day.

In John Jesus tells His disciples, "I have come so that they may have life and have it in abundance" (John 10:10). Life will not always be easy, as you well know, but we can experience a full and joyful life if God is the Lord of it. He will see you through the problems that come, and He will give you joy even in the midst of hardships. I encourage you to trust your life to Him.

LESSON 51

Prayer

The week of Buford's death, I underwent my second round of fertility tests, including my second HSG, all with favorable results. Then shortly after school dismissed for Christmas, I headed to Alabama for a visit with my grandmother and for some time of quiet and rest. This began a period of healing for me, and I started to feel the heaviness of the past few months lift a little. I also began laughing again, something I had not done in quite a while. However, I soon found myself stressing once more over having a child. The desire for a child grew strong within me, too strong probably because I became consumed with this desire. The weight of worry that had lifted came back, and I let it become even heavier than it had been before.

Around this time I went to visit my friend and we ate at a local pizza parlor. On the wall were many different sayings, thoughts for the day so to speak, most of them Christian in nature. Several of these caused me to reflect upon my attitude and how stressed I was about having a child. One of the sayings was about prayer: "When life is too tough to stand, kneel." Other sayings that I noticed posted on the wall were just single words, such as memories, prayer, laughter, and faith. As I thought about these words and quotes, a peace once again begin to fill me; and I decided on a theme or resolution for the upcoming year: prayer, laughter, and faith. Now I normally do not make New Year's resolutions, but these seemed appropriate because I knew these were all concepts with which I was struggling.

The first of these themes was prayer. While Lionel and I had been praying for over two years for a child, God showed me that we should continue praying and not give up. He reminded me of a story in the book of Luke that Jesus tells to teach His disciples the importance of persevering in prayer. In a town there was a widow who came before the judge asking for justice. The judge, who was not just and who really did not care about God or about people, kept brushing her aside; but the widow kept coming before him. Finally the judge got tired of the widow bothering him so he granted her request. Jesus tells His disciples that if this unjust judge granted justice to the widow just because she kept asking him, how much more will God grant justice to His children. Through this story He is teaching them (and us) that God will not put us off if we come before Him with faith (Luke 18:1–8).

How awesome to know that God listens to our prayers and answers them! The story of the persistent widow greatly encourages me. God will answer my prayers; I may just have to wait awhile for the answer, and I may have to be willing to take a "no" or a "not yet" as an answer. In the meantime I should continue to pray, and I must learn to adjust my prayers as God shows me so that my prayers fall in line with what He wants. I needed this reminder today as I write because even though I made up my mind that prayer was part of my theme for the year, just a few days ago I was discouraged. I wondered why I should continue to pray for a child when God does not seem to be answering. Just when I needed it, God has answered my prayer with a "wait" and a "keep praying." I praise God for giving me hope and for reminding me to persevere in prayer!

My Dear Reader, have you been praying for something for a long time? Are you tired of praying and ready to give up because God does not seem to hear or answer? Do not give up! First, examine your heart and life for sin; sin hinders our prayer. Is there any sin that you are harboring in your life, or are you walking in obedience to God? Second, examine your motives. James writes, "You ask and don't receive because you ask with wrong motives, so that you may spend it on your evil desires" (James 4:3). Are your motives pure? Are you truly seeking what God wants, or are you seeking your own pleasure and benefit?

Finally, pray. Pray and pray and pray some more. Paul writes to the Thessalonians, "Pray constantly" (1 Thess. 5:17). While I think Paul is referring more to having an attitude of prayer each day and to being in continual communication with God, I also think that this verse also applies here. Pray repeatedly throughout the day as your request or concern comes to mind.

If God has told you to pray for something, if He has brought someone or some situation to your mind and heart, "pray constantly." Pray and do not give up. Or as the acronym I have seen states, "PUSH: Pray Until Something Happens." Pray and expect God to answer. And remember that while His answer may not be what you expect, His answer is always best.

LESSON 52

Laughter

I have always been told that laughter is good medicine, and I believe that this is true. So many times laughter has been a healing balm for me. It relieves pain and it also helps relieve stress. I remember a very stressful period in college when I had had just about all that I could take. That evening my friends and I headed to a local hamburger joint for supper. I placed my order, picked it up, and proceeded to get some ketchup; but the ketchup dispenser was empty. I stood there mumbling to myself, "There's no ketchup; I think I'm going to cry." And I just about could have; that's how stressed I was! One of the workers happened to overhear me; and she said, "It's okay; I'll go get some ketchup." At that point I lost it, not crying from stress but laughing, laughing so hard that I was crying; once I started laughing, I could not stop. After my case of the giggles (as my mom and I call a good laughing fit), I was much less tense; the stress that I felt had gone away. Yes, I still had a lot to do but I had a much better attitude.

Another example of laughter helping me was after Buford's death. We had a cookie swap at church, and I started not to go; I just did not want to be social. However, at the last minute I decided to attend the cookie swap because I know that being around people is good for me. Mom and I sat together and had a good time talking and laughing. Now we did not get a good case of the giggles, but we did laugh a lot and had a wonderful time. In fact, one of the ladies at church commented on how much fun we seemed to have together. Going to the cookie swap that evening was one of the best choices that I could have made. Yes, I still needed more time to heal, but the laughter moved me a step forward.

My Dear Reader, life is too short to stay stressed and/or upset. Yes, bad things will happen, and yes, we need to deal with our emotions when they do; but take time to enjoy life. "Stop and smell the roses" as the saying goes. Laugh. Proverbs 17:22 says, "A joyful heart is good medicine." So lighten up. Enjoy life. Laugh out loud. Some may think you are crazy, but chances are you will bring a smile to someone else's face too; laughter tends to be contagious.

LESSON 53

Faith

F aith has been a struggle for me throughout my journey. I always thought I trusted God; but when the waiting and the hurt have been almost too much to bear, my faith was tested. There were times that I questioned God and His goodness, and I wondered whether prayer was worth the effort. I struggled to believe that God heard my prayers, much less answered them. In the midst of these questions and doubts, God pointed me to Hebrews 11.

Hebrews 11 is often referred to as the roll call of faith. The chapter begins with these words, "Now faith is the reality of what is hoped for, the proof of what is not seen" (Heb. 11:1). Then it continues by stating how faith pleases God: "Now without faith it is impossible to please God, for the one who draws near to Him must believe that He exists and rewards those who seek Him" (Heb. 11:6). The chapter goes on to name heroes of the faith and to tell their stories: Abel, Enoch, Noah, Abraham, Sarah, Isaac, Jacob, Joseph, Moses' parents, Moses, Rahab, and others. Finally, the chapter closes with these words, "All these were approved through their faith, but they did not receive what was promised, since God had provided something better for us, so that they would not be made perfect without us" (Heb. 11:39–40).

The words and stories from Hebrews 11 challenge me and cause me to examine my faith. Does my faith continue to show even though I have not yet received an answer to my prayers? Will I continue to trust that God has something better planned even if I do not understand the waiting, the hurt, and the disappointment in the meantime? Do I have a faith that pleases God? Do I believe that He will reward me for seeking Him? Am I truly seeking Him? These are the questions that I have to continually ask myself, and these are questions that you need to ask yourself as you travel your own journey of faith. Do you trust God? Do you believe that He will answer in a way that is best? Will you wait on Him?

Do you remember the parable of the persistent widow that I mentioned in Lesson 51? Jesus closed this parable with these words, "Nevertheless, when the Son of Man comes, will He find that faith on earth?" (Luke 18:8) Will Jesus find faith in you or have you given up hope? Faith is often hard for us so giving up is easy to do. We can pray; but when we do not see immediate answers, we begin to doubt. I know; I have been there. Throughout my journey of faith, I faced several crises of belief. These were the times that giving up seemed a better option than continuing to believe; but each time I doubted, God reassured me. Each time I faced questions such as "Am I going to continue to pray? Do I still trust God? Do I still believe that God will answer?", I came to the decision that yes, I will continue to pray, to believe, and to trust God. The road may not be easy and I may not yet have seen the answer to my prayers, but I know that God has something better planned and I have to hold onto that.

Just as faith itself is often difficult for us, the road over which faith leads us is not always easy. Just read Hebrews 11, and you will notice the struggles that these heroes of the faith faced and overcame. God never promised that life would be easy, but He did promise to be with us always, even to the end of time (Matt. 28:20). He also promised that nothing would be impossible for us if we had faith even as small as a mustard seed (Matt. 17:20). I do not know if you have ever seen a mustard seed, but it is small. If I am not mistaken, a mustard seed is one of the smallest seeds in the world. Jesus said that if we have faith, even this small, nothing will be impossible for us.

An old hymn is running through my mind now: "Have Faith in God." The hymn encourages us to have faith in God when we are lonely because He knows all that happens in our lives and because He will never leave us. It prompts us to trust God because He is sovereign, because He watches over us, and because He never fails. It tells us to believe God even when our prayers seem unanswered because He never forgets our prayers and because He always answers. It emboldens us to have faith in God despite our hurts and our worries because even though people and things around us fail, God never will.[1]

My Dear Reader, trust God. Have faith in Him. He will never let you down!

LESSON 54

Never Alone

One month in particular was a struggle due to grieving Buford's death, dealing with infertility, and battling my emotions related to both; but by the end of that month I was beginning to laugh again and starting to heal. I had hope as I remembered my theme for the new year. The next month, though, brought another downward spiral caused by the financial costs of all the fertility tests and the fact that our insurance would not cover those tests. Once again I found myself discouraged, struggling with faith, and even bitter. I remember wondering if my emotions were normal. Is the disappointment normal? Is the discouragement normal? Is the stress normal? Or is there something wrong with me? Life and my emotions seemed to be spinning out of control, and I had never felt so alone. For a period of time I felt like no one really understood what I was going through, that no one had been where I was. You see, infertility is the elephant in the room that people never mention. However, as I began to share with others about my struggles with infertility, I discovered that more and more women that I knew had also dealt with it; but until I spoke up, no one else did either.

Maybe you are faced with infertility or another elephant about which no one talks. Maybe you feel alone, more alone than you ever have in your life. No matter what your struggle is, you are not alone. First and foremost, God is always with you. In Matthew 28:20 Jesus promises to be with us always. Moses also states in Deuteronomy that

God would go with us and that He will never leave us nor forsake us (Deut. 31:6, 8). God is with you, no matter what you face. Second, there are people who have been where you are. Find a counselor or a support group if necessary; but there are people who do understand, who will listen, who will help, and who will offer comfort and advice. At the time I felt alone, I had forgotten about a friend at work to whom I had talked many times. She and her husband had struggled with infertility. She remembered the pain, the doubts, the tests, and the procedures. She recalled the emotional roller coaster which I was currently riding. She was a friend, a prayer partner, and a support during that lonely time. And as I mentioned in the previous paragraph, when I began talking more about the infertility that Lionel and I faced, I found many other women that I knew who had also struggled with infertility. Whatever problem you might have, there are other people who have faced the same problem or a similar situation; there are others who have hurt as you do, and they will pray for you. They will be there to listen to you and to support you.

Making you feel alone is one of Satan's tools. He wants you to feel alone so that you will become discouraged and be ineffective for God. The enemy wants to rob you of joy in any way that he can, and making you feel isolated steals away any hope or joy that you may have had. Do not fall into Satan's trap! My Dear Reader, you are never alone!

LESSON 55

Delighting in God

Delighting in God is one of the biggest lessons that God has taught me. I remember being down in the pit of emotion, and God speaking to me very clearly. He brought to mind Psalm 37:4: "Take delight in the Lord, and He will give you your heart's desires." In other words, God was telling me, "Heather, delight yourself in me; I promise to satisfy you and fulfill you. Be content with me." I am ashamed to say that for a period of time I had quit delighting in God. I wanted a child and I wanted a child badly, probably more than I wanted God. But God helped me realize that a child will never satisfy. A child can never complete me. A child will never fulfill me. Only God can do these things.

I could have chosen to continue to be worried, upset, and frustrated about not yet having a child; but the emotional turmoil was too great. I chose instead to delight myself in God, and I am much happier. My joy and my peace are restored. Are there still times when I hurt, when I struggle, and/or when I am disappointed? Yes, but I also know that ultimately God is what I need, and I have decided that I want Him more than anything else. I even want Him more than I want a child. I find pleasure in His presence and I long to spend time with Him. All of this is what delighting in God is.

Several years ago God gave me a new understanding of Psalm 37:4. The verse promises that God will fulfill your desires if you are delighting in Him. This promise is true because if you are delighting in God, then you are desiring Him; and if you are desiring Him and seeking Him, then He will come to you. In other words, if you are delighting in God, He can give you what you want because what you desire is Him.

In what are you delighting? Are you delighting in money? In clothes? In a job? In church? In a person? Or are you delighting in God? Remember that only He can completely satisfy and fulfill you. Only He will never, ever fail you. Learn to delight in Him. Be content with God and with all that He has given you. Bask in His great love. Find peace in Him, a peace that is beyond our understanding (Phil. 4:8).

My Dear Reader, "take delight in the Lord" (Ps. 37:4).

LESSON 56

God is Good

At one of my lowest points, a friend who had had trouble having a baby and had miscarried sent me an e-mail. She said that sometimes she thought about the baby she had lost; but when she did, she would also remember God's goodness. At the time that I received the e-mail, I was questioning God's goodness. How can I know that God is good? How can I know that God is good when I am hurting so deeply? How can I know that God is good when I see a world around me that is full of hurt and problems?

I began pondering God's goodness. I had always been told that God was good, and I had read in the Bible that God is good. But how do I KNOW God is good? Then I began thinking about all that God has done for me. He loved me so much that He sent His Son to die for me. He has forgiven me, and He continues to forgive me when I fail. He has provided for me; I have never lacked anything that I needed. He has healed me when I have been sick. He blessed me with a wonderful husband and with godly parents. I have a home, a job, and a car. Even the hardships that I have faced have always come out for the good; granted, they were not easy but God gave me strength to get through them. He taught me through the hardships, and in hindsight I recognize that His plan was always best. When I consider my life and all that God has done for me, I cannot help but realize and proclaim that God is good.

Psalm 34:8 says, "Taste and see that the Lord is good; how happy is the man who takes refuge in Him!" Psalm 86:5 states, "For You, Lord, are kind and ready to forgive, rich in faithful love to all who call on You." Psalm 119:68 declares, "You are good, and You do what is good; teach me Your statutes."

My Dear Reader, what about you? Have you realized that God is good? If you doubting God's goodness, begin making a list of all that He has done for you. Trust that God is good. Then bask in His love and in His goodness.

LESSON 57

Struggles as Teachable Moments

As I was learning to delight myself in God and as I was realizing God's goodness, God also reminded me that I needed to learn through the struggles I was facing, rather than just bellyaching about them. So I began praying and asking God to teach me; and well, I guess that was the beginning of this book. As you can see, God has taught me plenty; but I still have lots to learn.

My Dear Reader, our pain is never wasted. Remember that God is always working for the good of those who love Him; He uses the struggles that we face to purify us, to teach us, and to mold us into the men and women that He wants us to be. No, the struggles are never easy, and yes, the pain definitely hurts; but God is working.

What struggles are you facing? What is God trying to teach you? Be open to the lessons that He has for you. Pray as the psalmist did, "Teach us to number our days carefully so that we may develop wisdom in our hearts... Teach me, Lord, the meaning of Your statutes, and I will always keep them... Teach me to do Your will, for You are my God. May Your gracious Spirit lead me on level ground" (Ps. 90:12; 119:33; 143:10). Ask God what lessons you need to learn through your struggles; then have a heart that is willing to learn and ready for God to mold it.

LESSON 58

Letting Go of Bitterness

I think I mentioned this already, but our insurances had no infertility benefits which meant that all of the tests and all of the procedures were out-of-pocket expenses for us. This angered me tremendously because of the unfairness of the situation. I worked hard yet I did not receive the benefits that I needed. Every time I thought of this, I became angry all over again until I finally realized that I was carrying around bitterness. I was bitter toward the insurance company.

God commands us to let go of bitterness. Ephesians 4:31 states, "All bitterness, anger and wrath, shouting and slander must be removed from you, along with all malice." When I read this verse, I was cut to the heart because I realized the bitterness, the rage, and the anger that I was carrying around inside of me. I asked God to forgive me and to help me let go of the bitterness, and He did both.

God does not arbitrarily give us commands. His commands are always best so when God tells us to let go of bitterness, there is good reason for that. Bitterness eats away at our joy and peace; it makes us unpleasant people to be around, and sadly it hurts mostly just ourselves. Bitterness does not usually affect the one towards whom we are bitter. In my situation, the insurance company had no way of knowing that I was bitter towards them; I was hurting only myself by continuing to stay angry.

My Dear Reader, do not hang on to bitterness. Let go of the bitterness and the anger; leave them and your situation in God's hands. He will take care of you and of your hurt. Trust Him; you will be a lot happier if you do.

LESSON 59

Believing and Not Doubting

I mentioned that faith became one of my focuses; in fact, this whole book is about the journey of faith on which God led me. However, even though I decided to trust God and to have faith in Him, I have found that believing is often easier said than done. I have continually struggled with my faith, and many times I have faced questions about God. Am I going to believe God? Do I trust Him? Will I take Him at His Word? Do I have enough faith?

Maybe you are feeling the same way. A crisis of belief is a normal part of Christian growth. Questions and doubts lead us to search for answers and assurances; and when we turn to God for solutions, our faith grows as we see His responses. God promises, "You will seek Me and find Me when you search for Me with all your heart" (Jer. 29:13). He also promises, "Call to Me, and I will answer you and tell you great and incomprehensible things you do not know" (Jer. 33:3). When the questions and doubts arise (and they will), pray as the father in Mark did, "I do believe! Help my unbelief" (Mark 9:24).

Do not let your questions and doubts keep you from praying. Seek God during this time. Pray to Him; then choose to trust Him. Take up the shield of faith, and use it to extinguish the flaming arrows of doubt that Satan, our enemy, is throwing at you (Eph. 6:16).

My Dear Reader, choose to trust God; that is the best choice that you can make!

LESSON 60

Submitting to God

After the second round of unsuccessful fertility treatments, I faced another crisis of belief. Because I was hurt and disappointed, I really struggled with faith and prayer. I wondered why I should believe and why I should keep praying if God had seemingly not answered my prayers.

During this period in which I was wrestling with my faith, a team who had recently returned from a mission trip shared their testimonies in church—testimonies not about the trip itself but about what God had done for them and how they had developed a relationship with Him. These testimonies were a reminder to me about God's love, His goodness, and His power. One of my friends on the team shared how she did not know what God had planned for her children, but she did know that God's plans were always best. She quoted Jeremiah 29:11, "'For I know the plans I have for you,'—this is the Lord's declaration—'plans for your welfare, not for disaster, to give you a future and a hope.'" I needed this reminder that day because I did not comprehend God's plans. I did not understand why Lionel and I had prayed and believed and yet God still said wait; however, through the testimonies given that day, I remembered that God is good and that His plans are always best for us. Once again God knew just what I needed and He encouraged me. As I came to a crossroads in my crisis of belief, I decided to continue praying, to continue believing, and to continue trusting God for He plans to give me hope and a future. I chose to submit to God because

He always has my best interests at heart, because He has been faithful in the past, and because He will continue to be faithful.

Submitting to God is probably one of the hardest lessons to learn. Too many times we act like spoiled children. We want what we want when we want it. I know I found myself doing that. I wanted a child, I wanted one immediately, and I grumbled and complained when I did not get that child. However, I needed to learn to submit to God. He had already reminded me that His plan was best (Lesson 5), that His timing was perfect (Lesson 10), and that He does answer prayers (Lesson 1). He needed me to submit to His timing and His plan. I had to die to my own wishes.

In Luke Jesus tells His disciples, "If anyone wants to come with Me, he must deny himself, take up his cross daily, and follow Me" (Luke 9:23). If I am to go with Christ, then I have to deny myself. I have to lay aside what I want and trust God with my desires; I must trust Him to fill those desires in His way and in His time. If I am to go with Christ, I need to take up my cross daily. For me taking up my cross is enduring the fertility struggles and handing my desire for child over to God. It necessitates dying to myself and finding my fulfillment and satisfaction in God. It means delighting myself in Him. Finally if I am to go with Christ, then I must follow Him; I must walk with Him each day. This entails spending time reading His Word, studying His Word, talking to Him, and listening to Him. It involves obeying Him no matter what He asks of me. Following Jesus requires living my life for His glory and not for my own pleasure.

My Dear Reader, submitting to God is not easy but it is always best. Remember God is working for the good of His children (Rom. 8:28) and He has a plan for your success (maybe not success as most people define it but success nonetheless) and not for your harm, a plan to give you hope and a future (Jer. 29:11). And while God's way is not always the easiest (in fact, it is often quite difficult), you will find great joy, peace, and satisfaction—joy, peace, and satisfaction that cannot be found anywhere else—when you follow His will. "Therefore, submit to God..." (James 4:7)

LESSON 61

God's Provision

For those of you who may not know this, fertility treatments are quite expensive. The total cost for us was around $1500 each month. Yet despite these expenses, God graciously provided for Lionel and me throughout this period. Yes, there were some lean times and we had to make decisions to cut spending where we could; but as we prayed that God would take care of us, we never lacked for anything that we truly needed.

For example, in the middle of the treatments we had trouble with our heat, and this was in the winter when we needed the heat. Sometimes the heat would work and sometimes it would not, but we figured out how to get it working again anytime it quit. The "repairs" only cost a little over $50 when we were expecting a bigger job of several hundred to a thousand dollars. I saw this as God's provision. I had prayed many times when our heat was acting up that God would provide for us to pay both for having the heat fixed and for the fertility treatments, and He did.

I have many more stories from when I was in graduate school or just out of school trying to make ends meet and God provided for my financial needs. Sometimes a tank of gas lasted longer than it should have. One time I got just the amount of money I needed in a raise. Other times my parents would leave a $20 bill after their visit even though I had not mentioned that I needed money.

I have no doubt that God has provided for me financially, and I am ashamed to say that during our treatments and our heat problems there were times that I worried that we would be able to make ends meet. At those times I had to ask God's forgiveness for worrying, and then I told Him our needs and asked Him to provide. And He did!

Paul writes in Philippians 4:19, "And my God will supply all your needs according to His riches in glory in Christ Jesus." Notice this verse does not say that God will meet some of your needs; it says, "God will supply *ALL* [emphasis mine] your needs." If you have a need, tell God that need and ask Him to provide for you. Then trust Him to work in a way that only He can. Listen to His direction; maybe what you thought was a need was really only a want. Or maybe what you saw as a need developed because of unwise spending on your part. Be willing to make adjustments as God leads because sometimes His giving us wisdom in our spending is the means that He uses to provide for us. Other times, He provides in ways you could never imagine.

My Dear Reader, trust God to take care of you; rest in His provision.

LESSON 62

Counting Your Blessings

Getting wrapped up in your problem(s) and forgetting the good things that you have in your life is easy to do. When Lionel or I are having a bad day, one of the things we ask each other is "What are three things for which you are thankful?" Stopping to think about the answer to this question usually helps us to refocus and to remember how blessed we are. This activity shifts our focus from ourselves back to God, and it helps improve our attitudes.

God reminded me recently to count my blessings. Yes, I am hurt and disappointed that we do not yet have a child, but I really do have so much for which to be thankful. On one of the days that I was really struggling—hurting because of the infertility and worrying about money—I opened the refrigerator and saw that it was full of food. I do not think we could have stuffed anything else in the fridge! I realized just how blessed I was! I recalled that I have a beautiful home, a wonderful husband, a car that gets me from point A to point B dependably, a job that I enjoy (well, most days at least ☺), a family that loves me, friends that support me and pray for me, a church family that is dear to me, and many more blessings—more than I can name. My cup overflows! I also remembered that while we may not yet have a child I am a child of God, and that is the biggest blessing ever! God has adopted us as His children, and nothing can take us out of His hands. He loves us and He forgives us. God takes care of us. He gives us joy, peace, hope, and strength. He comforts us, encourages us, heals us, and helps us. He provides for us and He protects us. He is always with us.

When life beats you down, take a minute or two to count your blessings. Learn to live with an attitude of gratitude rather than one of grumbling. Paul writes in 1 Thessalonians 5:18 that we are to "give thanks in everything, for this is God's will for you in Christ Jesus." This does not mean that we have to be thankful for the struggles we face and the hurt we feel, but it does imply that in the midst of the problems and the pain, we still thank God for what He has done for us. This shifts our focus from ourselves to God, and it reminds us that ultimately He is sovereign over our problems.

An old hymn entitled "Count Your Blessings" encourages us to count our blessings in the midst of our problems and our discouragement. When we do, we will be surprised and emboldened as we remember all that God has done for us. As we count our blessings, our doubts and worries begin to ease because we remember that God is ultimately in charge. The hymn reminds us not to envy what others have but to be satisfied because God has given us so much.[1]

I keep a gratitude journal, and each day I write something for which I am thankful. Usually that something is small, but taking time to write down at least one blessing each day has made a huge difference in my attitude. I worry less and smile more when I write in my gratitude journal.

My Dear Reader, I encourage you to count your blessings and to "give thanks to the Lord, for He is good; His faithful love endures forever" (Ps. 107:1).

LESSON 63

Waiting on the Lord

Waiting is never easy. We are such impatient people. We have a microwave that can finish a meal in two to three minutes, fast food restaurants that give us our orders in under five minutes, and even Express Check-Outs so that we can get through the line quickly. We do not want to wait; we desire immediate gratification. However, waiting on God is always best.

When Lionel and I first decided to have a child, we thought that I would get pregnant immediately so you can imagine how discouraging waiting several years for a child has been. I am ashamed to say that so many times I have acted like a little girl because I wanted a child and I wanted one now. I have wondered why God would give us a desire for a child yet not satisfy that desire. However, I come back to realizing that God's timing is always best. Earlier lessons reminded me that He is in control (Lesson 6), that His timing is perfect (Lesson 10), that He is working for our good (Lesson 5), and that He has a plan to prosper us and to give us hope (Lesson 5).

As I write this, Lionel and I continue our waiting. We just had our third round of fertility treatments, and now we just have to hurry up and wait to see if they worked. The treatments have been a series of two to three week waits. The waiting has not been easy; but as I wait, I look back on all that I have written so far. God has taught me and reminded me of so many lessons through this waiting period. He has drawn me closer to Him; and if I had not had the wait, I am not sure that this would have happened. So, yes, waiting is difficult (no matter what you are waiting for), but God is faithful and He will be with you through the waiting.

Are you waiting for a child like we are? Are you waiting for a husband? Are you waiting for the results of a medical test? Whatever you are waiting for, God already knows the answer and the timing, and He is teaching you. Remember Lesson 57? Ask God to teach you through the struggles and through the waiting. Ask Him to be with you and to draw you close as you wait. Ask Him to give you the faith that you need to believe as you wait. My Dear Reader, He will do all these and more.

I was nearly thirty years old when Lionel and I married. I had waited a long time for God to bring the right man into my life, and I guarantee that he was worth the wait. And as we wait now for a child, I am excited to see what God is going to do and how He will answer our prayers; I know that this, too, will be well worth the wait.

Psalm 27:14 has been encouraging to me through the waiting periods of my life, such as waiting for a husband and waiting for a child. This verse says, "Wait for the Lord; be strong and courageous. Wait for the Lord." My Dear Reader, take heart; be encouraged. God has your best interests in mind, and He is able to do so much more than we could ever imagine (Eph. 3:20). Be strong. Look to God and find your strength in Him as you wait. Seek Him and cling to Him. Wait for the Lord; His timing and His ways are perfect.

LESSON 64

Peace that Passes Understanding

When Lionel and I underwent our third and final fertility treatment, God's peace flooded my heart on the drive back home. This was just one of many times over the last few years that God has blessed me with peace in the midst of the hurting, the longing, and the waiting. This peace is a peace that is beyond my understanding, a peace that I could not begin to describe in words. It is a peace that begins with knowing that even though we have had a long road to travel, God is sovereign over all that has happened. It is a peace that is founded on recognizing that God is aware of everything in my life and that He has control of every circumstance and situation. It is a peace that develops from realizing that I do not have to understand everything that happens and why God allows it; I just have to trust Him.

Paul writes, "Don't worry about anything, but in everything through prayer and petition with thanksgiving, let your requests be made known to God. And the peace of God, which surpasses every thought, will guard your hearts and minds in Christ Jesus" (Phil. 4:6–7). If you are worried about some problem you are facing and/or if you are hurt, lay the situation at God's feet. Tell Him what is bothering you, what you need, and even what you want; then let Him carry that burden for you. Let Him heal you. Rest in God; trust Him and His peace will flood your life. If the enemy attacks and robs you of this peace, then lay your request at God's feet again and again and again; anytime that it is o your mind, turn it over to God and shift your mind to God. H

12:2 says, "…keeping our eyes on Jesus, the source and perfecter of our faith, who for the joy that lay before Him endured a cross and despised the shame and has sat down at the right hand of God's throne." Your eyes should not be fixed on the problem that lies in your path; your eyes should be fixed on the God Who is bigger than that problem.

Paul continues in Philippians 4, "Finally, brothers, whatever is true, whatever is honorable, whatever is just, whatever is pure, whatever is lovely, whatever is commendable—if there is any moral excellence and if there is any praise—dwell on these things" (Phil. 4:8). Paul tells the Corinthians and the Colossians the same things but with different words. He says to consciously take hold of every thought and to fix our minds on Christ (2 Cor. 10:5; Col. 3:1–2). I cannot tell you how many times I have had to do this. I start to worry about having a child, and I let the enemy rob me of my joy and my peace. However, God reminds me to think about good things, pure things, lovely things, excellent things, true things, and praiseworthy things. I realize that I need to think not about myself and my situation but about God. I consciously take hold of my thoughts and refocus them on God. I pray and I lay my worries in God's hands, and then I let His peace fill my heart.

Now is one of those times I have to do this. As I write, my fellow Phi Theta Kappa advisors are in California at the International Convention. I have never been to California and I love traveling with my fellow advisors and my students; but because of the fertility treatments, I was unable to go. I could be all mad and upset (and trust me I have been at times), but I have chosen to be happy for them, to fix my mind on Jesus, and to count the blessings of staying home. Is this easy? No. Do I still wish I was in California? Yes. However, I prayed about going to California, and God told me not to go. While I miss being with my friends, ʳ ing new places, and having adventures, amazingly God's pᵉ ʳ as I consciously make every thought obedient to Christ.

ʳeader, learn to practice this. Learn to focus on the good
vour blessings, and to fix your mind on God. Learn to
s captive rather than letting them take you captive.
ʋu rest in the Father's tender love and care, you will
ʳhat passes understanding.

LESSON 65

Listening to Satan's Lies

L istening to Satan's lies is a problem that I have faced again and again. Satan, our enemy, lied to me and tried to convince me that I am defective since I have not been able to conceive. (In fact, several times along my journey I apologized to Lionel that he married a defective wife.) Through this lie Satan attacked my worth and my sense of value. However, I have learned to put on the belt of truth (Eph. 6:14) by reading and studying God's Word. I cling to Scripture tightly for it is truth. I also wear the helmet of salvation (Eph. 6:17). Through Jesus God rescued me from sin; and rather than think on the lies that Satan tries to feed me, I consciously think about God, His Word, and the good things that He has given me.

My Dear Reader, ground yourself in God's Word for His Word is truth (Ps. 119:138,142). His Word is righteous and pure (Ps. 119:140,144), and it endures forever (Isa. 40:8). Intentionally focus on God's Word rather than on the lies that Satan feeds you. If Satan tries to convince you that you are defective, remember that the Bible says that you are "remarkably and wonderfully made" and that God's "works are wonderful" (Ps. 139:14). If Satan tries to tell you that you are not valuable, remember that God chose you to be His own (Deut. 7:6); you are precious to Him. If Satan tries to convince you that you are not talented or gifted in any way, remember that the Spirit gives each of us different gifts (1 Cor. 12:4–11); search out what gift(s) you have, and ask God to show you what your areas of ministry are. Whatever lies Satan tries to feed you, there are truths in God's Word to combat those lies.

Stop listening to Satan's lies! Take up the sword of the Spirit—God's Word—and stand firm in God and in His truths (Eph. 6:13–14,17).

LESSON 66

Negative Self-talk

T his lesson goes right along with the previous one. Do not believe or even listen to Satan's lies, but also do not embark in negative self-talk. This is a habit that I have found myself having fallen into over the last several months.

As Lionel and I struggled with infertility, I felt defective and I had to really fight hard not to believe this lie. I have also been calling myself a dweeb or a geek because of something I did. Sometimes I did this jokingly, but other times I really felt like I was a dweeb or a geek. As I was lying in bed last night, I realized the dangers of this. If I call myself bad names, I might eventually believe it; and this is just where Satan wants me. He wants me to start feeling badly about myself so that I am not meeting my full potential in the Lord, so that I am not doing all that God wants me to do, and so that I am not as effective for the kingdom.

The psalmist writes, "For it was You who created my inmost parts; You knit me together in my mother's womb. I will praise You because I have been remarkably and wonderfully made. Your works are wonderful, and I know this very well" (Ps. 139:13–14). God created you and His works are wonderful. You are made in His image (Gen. 1:27), and you have been chosen by Him (Col. 3:12). You are greatly loved (Col. 3:12).

Just like we should not talk bad about other people, we also should not talk bad about ourselves. Please understand that I am not saying you need to go around patting yourself on the back and saying how great you are; that is pride. But you also should not put yourself down. Learn to love yourself.

My Dear Reader, "you are a chosen race, a royal priesthood, a holy nation, a people for His possession, so that you may proclaim the praises of the One who called you out of darkness into His marvelous light" (1 Peter 2:9).

LESSON 67

Complaining

Complaining is another area in which God has been working in me. The lesson has come slowly but surely as thoughts hanging around in my mind until the thoughts have gelled into a lesson.

Complaining is so easy to do. Poor pitiful me because I have too much to do. Poor pitiful me because I have a huge problem to face. Poor pitiful me because... fill in the blank. Our human nature is to focus on self and to complain, but we have so much for which to be thankful.

Philippians 2:14 – 16 says, "Do everything without grumbling and arguing so that you may be blameless and pure, children of God who are faultless in a crooked and perverted generation, among whom you shine like stars in the world. Hold firmly to the message of life." If you are complaining, you are not holding "firmly to the message of life." If you are complaining, life has become about you and not about God. If you are complaining, you are not shining like a star.

In Numbers 13 – 14 the Israelites missed a great blessing when they grumbled and complained. They were on the edge of entering the Promised Land; however, they chose to grumble rather than trust God, and God told them that everyone who was twenty years old or older would die in the desert. Everyone who had grumbled against God would not enter the Promised Land (Num. 14:29–30). The only ones who entered the Promised Land were Joshua and Caleb because they did not grumble against God; they trusted Him.

My Dear Reader, grumbling not only dishonors God, but it keeps us from missing a bigger blessing that God may have in store for us. So instead of grumbling and complaining, live with an attitude of gratitude. "This is the day that the Lord has made; let us rejoice and be glad in it" (Ps. 118:24).

LESSON 68

All about God

Throughout my writing, this has been a lesson about which God was reminding me. As I have written each day, my focus has shifted from me and my problems to where my focus needs to be—God. I once heard a preacher state, "It's all about Jesus," and that statement has stuck with me since I heard his sermon. Life is not about me, what I can do, what I accomplish, or the problems that I face; my life should be centered on God. It should point to Him and not to me.

Paul writes, "Therefore, whether you eat or drink, or whatever you do, do everything for God's glory" (1 Cor. 10:31). And in Matthew Jesus tells His disciples, "In the same way, let your light shine before men, so that they may see your good works and give glory to your Father in heaven" (Matt. 5:16). My Dear Reader, while this lesson is short, it is important. All that we think, all that we do, and all that we say should bring glory to God. Is your life pointing to God or is it pointing to you? Remember, life is not about you; it is all about God.

LESSON 69

Clothed with Humility

As I remembered that life is all about Jesus and not about me, God also reminded me that humility is a trait that characterizes His children. This is another short yet important lesson.

Peter writes, "And all of you clothe yourselves with humility toward one another, because God resists the proud but gives grace to the humble. Humble yourselves, therefore, under the mighty hand of God, so that He may exalt you at the proper time, casting all your care on Him, because He cares for you" (1 Peter 5:5–7). To humble yourself means that less of yourself is showing and more of God is shining through. It implies thinking not less of yourself but less often of yourself. It suggests learning to see yourself as God sees you. Humbling yourself is not putting yourself down, rather it is not drawing attention to yourself. It involves bringing God glory and leaving your life in His hands. Humbling yourself means putting aside your desires and serving others; it requires putting others before yourself (Phil. 2:3–4). Ultimately, it entails following Jesus' example, living as He lived, and seeking to glorify the Father (Phil. 2:5–8).

My Dear Reader, be clothed with humility.

LESSON 70

Walking by Faith

Walking by faith is the primary lesson that God has been teaching me through the last few years. This idea has been germinating for a little while in the back of my mind, but God brought it forward today in my devotional.

Paul writes in 2 Corinthians 5:7, "For we walk by faith, not by sight." No, Lionel and I do not yet have an answer to our prayers for a child, and yes, this means we are still waiting; but through it all, we live by faith—trusting God to do what is best and trusting His perfect timing. We live by faith rather than by sight because we do not yet see the answer. And I am okay with that. God has a plan that He will fulfill in His timing and in His way, and we will trust Him. We will trust Him if His answer is yes. We will trust Him if His answer is wait. We will trust Him if His answer is no. Beyond that we will praise Him, now as we wait and later when we have our answer, no matter what that answer is.

Paul continues His thought in 2 Corinthians 5, "For we walk by faith, not by sight, and we are confident and satisfied to be out of the body and at home with the Lord. Therefore, whether we are at home or away, we make it our aim to be pleasing to Him" (2 Cor. 5:7–9). My Dear Reader, no matter where your journey of faith takes you, no matter what lies on the road ahead, make it your goal to please God. Delight yourself in Him and live by faith rather than by sight.

Final Lesson

The Road to Heaven

My Dear Reader, I have told you about my most recent travels on my journey of faith, but this journey began when I was nine years old. I made a decision that changed the rest of my life. I made a decision to follow Jesus.

First, I realized that I was a sinner. Sin is doing wrong; it is disobeying God. The Bible tell us that we are all sinners and that there is no one who is perfect (Rom. 3:10,23). Our sin separates us from God because He is holy (Ps. 99:3,5).

Second, I learned that sin has a price. Romans 6:23 tells us that the penalty for sin is death. Death, here, is two-fold: physical death (God took Adam and Eve out of the Garden of Eden when they disobeyed Him so that they could not eat from the tree of life and live forever (Gen. 3:22–24)) and spiritual death (separation from God and an eternity spent in hell).

Third, I discovered that there is hope. Jesus died on the cross, paying our sin debt. Romans 5:8 states, "But God proves His own love for us in that while we were still sinners Christ died for us!" Romans 6:23 says that God's gift to us is eternal life through His Son. Eternal life is a gift for us to accept not a token for us to earn (Eph. 2:8–9). We cannot do enough good to get us into heaven because our sin taints all of the good things that we do (Isa. 64:6). However, we can turn to Jesus; He will forgive us (1 John 1:9) and make us as white as snow (Isa. 1:18).

Then we will go to heaven when we die (or when Jesus comes back, whichever comes first). This is salvation.

Last, I talked to God. I admitted that I was a sinner and that I needed Him. I told Him that I believed that Jesus is His Son and that Jesus died on the cross for my sin. I expressed to God my sorrow for my sins, and I asked Him to help me change so that I would do what is right. I spoke to Him of my desire to be with Him in heaven. Finally, I stated that I gave God control of my life.

My Dear Reader, I cannot leave without asking you several questions. Do you know who Jesus is? Beyond that, do you know Him as Savior? When you die, will you go to heaven, not because of your good works but because of God's gift of eternal life? If you cannot answer these questions with a resounding and certain "Yes!", then I encourage you to call on the name of the Lord and experience His salvation (Rom. 10:13). Jesus stands at the door of your heart, and He is knocking and waiting for you to invite Him into your life (Rev. 3:20). This is the best and the most important decision you could ever make.

If today you have made a decision to follow Jesus and begin your own journey of faith, I would love to hear about that decision. You can contact me through e-mail at faithjourney@outlook.com. Also I encourage you to contact your local church (or find a Bible-believing, God-fearing church near you), and let them know the decision that you have made. They will support you and encourage you on your journey.

Farewell!

I come to the end of my writing for now. I have taken you through the last few years and the lessons that God has taught me. I have also shared with you what God has done for me. I hope that through this journey together you have seen not me but God, and I pray that He has encouraged you through what you have read.

We come to the end of this journey together, but the journey of faith continues for a lifetime. There are many more lessons ahead, much more that we need to learn, more that God wants to teach us. We are His pupils. Teach us, Father; may our hearts be ever listening to You and learning from You.

"Now faith is the reality of what is hoped for, the proof of what is not seen" (Heb. 11:1).

"Now to Him Who is able to do above and beyond all that we ask or think according to the power that works in us—to Him be glory in the church and in Christ Jesus to all generations, forever and ever. Amen" (Eph. 3:20).

Study Guide

F
rom my teaching and general life experiences, I have learned that reading something is usually not enough for us to take lessons to heart. Below are listed the Scriptures that occurred in each lesson along with a thought or two to stimulate further reflection. My prayer is that this Study Guide takes you further along on your personal journey of faith.

Lesson 1: Answered Prayers

Scripture References: 1 Samuel 1–2; 1 Kings 3–4; 18; Psalm 3:4; 4:3; 5:3; 6:9; 10:17; Isaiah 38; Jonah 1–2; Matthew 18:19–20; 21:21–22; Hebrews 4:16; 1 John 5:14–15

For Further Reflection: Name prayers that God has answered for you, and thank Him for those answers.

Lesson 2: When There Seems To Be No Answer

Scripture References: Isaiah 55:8–9; Matthew 18:19–20; 21:18–22; Hebrews 4:16; James 1:5–7; 4:2,3; 1 John 5:14–15

For Further Reflection: Do you have a prayer that seems unanswered? Have you talked to God about this concern? Are your motives proper? Are you praying for God's will or for your own desires? Do you truly believe that God will answer your prayer?

Lesson 3: The God of All Comfort

Scripture Reference: 2 Corinthians 1:3–4

For Further Reflection: Is there someone whom you need to comfort and/or encourage? How can you use your past experiences to help others?

Lesson 4: Pouring Out Your Heart

Scripture Reference: Psalm 62:8

For Further Reflection: Are you currently hurting or angry? Have your poured out your heart to God? Will you trust Him with your emotions?

Lesson 5: Working for Our Good

Scripture References: Jeremiah 29:11; Romans 8:28

For Further Reflection: What bad situation have you faced that God used for good? What other evidence have you seen of God's working for your good?

Lesson 6: God Is in Control

Scripture References: Job 25:2; Psalm 22:28; 31:15; 33:11; Proverbs 16:4; 19:21

For Further Reflection: Are you trying to control your own life or are you following God? If you are currently facing a troubling circumstance, did you cause it by doing what was wrong or has God allowed this problem to teach you?

Lesson 7: Parents Must Be Intentional

Scripture Reference: Deuteronomy 6:6–7

For Further Reflection: If you are a parent or guardian, how are you intentionally teaching your children about God?

Lesson 8: Christians as Ambassadors

Scripture References: Deuteronomy 6:6–9; Matthew 5:16; 2 Corinthians 5:20; Colossians 4:6

For Further Reflection: Are you a good ambassador for God, appropriately representing Him? Are your words honoring God? Is your life pure, radiating Jesus' love through your actions? Do you tell others what He has done for you?

Lesson 9: Draw Close Together

Scripture Reference: Genesis 2

For Further Reflection: How do you and your spouse handle difficulties? Do you withdraw from each other or do you draw close together? Do you spout out angry words or do you try to support and encourage each other?

Lesson 10: God's Perfect Timing
Scripture Reference: Ecclesiastes 3:11

For Further Reflection: When have you had to wait on God? What did God teach you through the waiting? What was the end result of the waiting?

Lesson 11: Heaven
Scripture References: John 14:1–3; Philippians 1:21–24; Revelation 21–22

For Further Reflection: Read Revelation 21–22 and describe heaven in your own words.

Lesson 12: The God of All Comfort
Scripture References: Psalm 62:8; John 11:1–44; 2 Corinthians 1:3; Philippians 4:7

For Further Reflection: How has God comforted you through trials both past and present?

Lesson 13: Have Faith
Scripture References: Jeremiah 29:11; Mark 9:17–24; Luke 17:6; Ephesians 3:20–21; Hebrews 11

For Further Reflection: Read Hebrews 11; describe which "hero" impresses you the most and why.

Lesson 14: God Heals Our Hurts
Scripture References: Matthew 8:1–17,28–34; 9:1–8,20–22,27–34; 15:21–28; 17:14–23; 20:29–34; 1 Peter 5:10

For Further Reflection: How has God healed you in the past—physically, emotionally, spiritually, and/or mentally? Or how is He healing you now?

Lesson 15: Stuffing Away Emotions

Scripture References: Psalm 62:8; Galatians 5:22–23

For Further Reflection: Do you have any emotions from which you are trying to run away? With whom can you share your feelings, and whom can you trust to pray for you? Have you shared your emotions with God?

Lesson 16: Enjoy the Memories

Scripture References: Exodus 11–13; Joshua 3–4

For Further Reflection: What good memories do you cherish? What are some amazing things that God has done for you, things that you can remember when life gets tough?

Lesson 17: Bad Memories

Scripture References: Romans 8:28; 1 Corinthians 11:23–26

For Further Reflection: Name some positive things that God brought out of a bad situation that you faced.

Lesson 18: Ask for Help

Scripture References: Ecclesiastes 4:9–12; John 15:5; Galatians 6:2–3

For Further Reflection: With what do you currently need help? How can you help someone else?

Lesson 19: Open Eyes

Scripture References: Matthew 25:14–30; 28:19–20; Acts 1:8

For Further Reflection: Are your eyes open to opportunities that God gives you to tell others about Him? What opportunities do you currently see?

Lesson 20: Opportunities

Scripture References: Matthew 8:12; Ephesians 5:15–16; Revelation 20:15

For Further Reflection: Are you looking for opportunities to speak of God, and are you making the most of each opportunity?

Lesson 21: A Willing Vessel

Scripture References: 2 Corinthians 9:8; Ephesians 3:20; Philippians 4:19; 2 Timothy 3:16–17; Hebrews 13:21

For Further Reflection: Are you a willing vessel? Are you going to step out in faith and do whatever God asks you to do whenever He asks you to do it?

Lesson 22: A Higher Standard

Scripture Reference: James 3:1

For Further Reflection: How thoroughly do you know God's Word? Do your words and actions match? Whom has God entrusted to your care, and how well are you teaching them God's ways?

Lesson 23: Spiritual Warfare

Scripture References: 2 Samuel 5:23–24; 2 Kings 6:8–23; Daniel 10:12–13; John 8:44; 10:10; 2 Corinthians 10:3–4; Ephesians 6:10–18; 1 Peter 5:8; Jude 9

For Further Reflection: How aware of you of spiritual warfare? Are you grounded in God and His Word? Have you put on your spiritual armor?

Lesson 24: The Fight Against Satan

Scripture Reference: Ephesians 6:12

For Further Reflection: Whom are you fighting—God, people, or the devil?

Lesson 25: Called to Pray

Scripture Reference: James 5:13–16

For Further Reflection: For whom has God called you to pray? Are you praying for that person or persons?

Lesson 26: Two or Three Sides to Every Story

Scripture References: Proverbs 18:8; 19:2; 26:22

For Further Reflection: To what conclusions have you jumped? What was the result?

Lesson 27: Divorce

Scripture Reference: Mark 10:1–12

For Further Reflection: Do you know someone in the middle of a divorce or recovering from a divorce? How can you be an encouragement to that person? How can you best pray for him/her?

Lesson 28: The Valleys of Questions and Waiting

Scripture References: Deuteronomy 31:6,8; Jeremiah 29:11

For Further Reflection: What questions do you have? Have you asked God those questions? Are you willing to trust Him for the answers in His time and in His way?

Lesson 29: The Story of Job

Scripture References: Job 1–42; Joel 2:25; 2 Corinthians 1:4; Hebrews 12:3–11

For Further Reflection: What is your response to trials? Do you whine and complain, or do you turn to God and trust Him?

Lesson 30: Will I Trust God?

Scripture References: Genesis 12; 16; 21; 25:20–26; 29:31–30:24; 35:16–18; 1 Samuel 1–2; Job 38–41; Proverbs 3:5–6; Luke 1

For Further Reflection: What problem(s) are you currently facing? Will you trust God with those problems?

Lesson 31: Is God Enough?

Scripture References: Psalm 90:14; 103; 145:16; Isaiah 55:1–2

For Further Reflection: What is your greatest desire, your deepest longing? Have you given God that desire? Do you trust Him to satisfy you?

Lesson 32: Will I Walk Away from God?

Scripture References: Psalm 73:25–26; John 6:60–69

For Further Reflection: Are you willing to follow God even if what He asks you to do is difficult? Are you willing to trust God no matter what?

Lesson 33: Extending Grace and Love

Scripture References: John 3:16; 13:34–35; Romans 3:23; 5:8; 2 Corinthians 5:20–21; 2 Timothy 2:1; 1 John 4:11,19

For Further Reflection: To whom is God calling you to extend grace and love? How can you best show God's grace and love to that person?

Lesson 34: Reacting in Anger

Scripture References: Proverbs 15:1; 22:24; 29:11,22; 1 Corinthians 13; Galatians 5:22–23; Ephesians 4:26–32; Philippians 4:7; James 1:19

For Further Reflection: Would you describe yourself as a patient person, or are you easily angered? Do you turn to God when you are angry, or do you react without thinking or praying?

Lesson 35: Witnesses

Scripture References: John 14:15–26; 15:18–25; 16:1–15; Acts 1:8; 5; 7; 8:1–4; 12; Romans 14:12; 2 Corinthians 11; Philippians 3:20; 1 Thessalonians 4:13–18; 2 Timothy 1:7; Hebrews 4:13; James 4:13–14; 1 Peter 2:11; 2 Peter 3:1–13

For Further Reflection: How often do you tell others about God's salvation? With whom can you share the gospel?

Lesson 36: Love One Another

Scripture References: John 13:34–35; Galatians 5:22–23; Philippians 2:6–11

For Further Reflection: Do you love others as God has loved you? Do you love selflessly? Do you love unconditionally? Do you love sacrificially?

Lesson 37: Extend Grace

Scripture References: 2 Corinthians 1:3–4; Ephesians 3:20; Philippians 4:7,19; James 5:15; 1 John 1:9

For Further Reflection: Is there a troublesome situation in your life today in which grace needs to be exhibited?

Lesson 38: Forgive

Scripture References: Psalm 103:12; Micah 7:19; Matthew 18:21–35; Ephesians 4:32

For Further Reflection: Whom do you need to forgive?

Lesson 39: Better To Give Than To Receive

Scripture Reference: Acts 20:35

For Further Reflection: How much and to whom does God want you to give? What is He asking you to give? Time? Money? A kind word?

Lesson 40: God Answers Prayer

Scripture References: Psalm 3:4; Ephesians 3:20

For Further Reflection: How has God answered your prayers?

Lesson 41: Friendship

Scripture References: Proverbs 17:17; 18:24; 27:10

For Further Reflection: To whom do you need to be a friend?

Lesson 42: Being a Servant

Scripture References: Mark 10:35–45; Acts 20:35

For Further Reflection: Whom is God calling you to serve? In what way?

Lesson 43: Difficult Decisions

Scripture References: 1 Corinthians 4:1–2; 1 Peter 4:10

For Further Reflection: Have you discussed end-of-life decisions with your family? Have you discussed future health care with your family?

Lesson 44: Just What You Need

Scripture References: Psalm 10:17; 2 Corinthians 1:3

For Further Reflection: Name a time when God gave you just what you needed. Thank Him for doing so.

Lesson 45: God in the Small Things

Scripture References: 1 Kings 19:9–18; Ephesians 3:20

For Further Reflection: When have you seen God in the small things of life?

Lesson 46: Praying for Direction

Scripture References: Romans 11:33; James 1:5

For Further Reflection: In what situation do you currently need direction? Have you asked God for wisdom?

Lesson 47: Take Care of Yourself

Scripture Reference: 1 Corinthians 6:19–20

For Further Reflection: Are you taking care of yourself? Do you eat nutritiously? Do you exercise regularly? Are you getting the rest that you need?

Lesson 48: Abortion

Scripture References: Exodus 20:13; Psalm 139:13,14; Jeremiah 1:5

For Further Reflection: Take a moment to reflect on the sanctity of life.

Lesson 49: Strength When We Need It

Scripture References: Exodus 15:2; Nehemiah 8:10; Psalm 18:1,32; 28:7; 46:1; 118:14; Isaiah 40:30–31

For Further Reflection: Describe a time when God has given you strength (i.e, emotional strength, physical strength, spiritual strength).

Lesson 50: Life and Death

Scripture References: Psalm 116:15; John 10:10

For Further Reflection: Are enjoying the moments that God gives you? Are you making the most of each opportunity? Are you living life to the fullest while staying within God's boundaries?

Lesson 51: Prayer

Scripture References: Luke 18:1–8; 1 Thessalonians 5:17; James 4:3

For Further Reflection: For what have you been praying for a long time? Have you examined your heart for sin? Have you examined your motives for purity?

Lesson 52: Laughter

Scripture Reference: Proverbs 17:22

For Further Reflection: How often do you laugh? When was the last time you laughed?

Lesson 53: Faith

Scripture References: Matthew 17:20; 28:20; Luke 18:8; Hebrews 11

For Further Reflection: Do you trust God? Do you believe that He will answer your prayers in a way that is best?

Lesson 54: Never Alone

Scripture References: Deuteronomy 31:6,8; Matthew 28:20

For Further Reflection: Do you feel alone? Ask God to show you someone with whom you can share your struggles.

Lesson 55: Delighting in God

Scripture References: Psalm 37:4; Philippians 4:8

For Further Reflection: In what are you delighting? Are you delighting in money? In clothes? In a job? In church? In a person? Or are you delighting in God?

Lesson 56: God Is Good

Scripture References: Psalm 34:8; 86:5; 119:68

For Further Reflection: Make a list of all that God has done for you and ponder His goodness.

Lesson 57: Struggles as Teachable Moments

Scripture References: Psalm 90:12; 119:33; 143:10

For Further Reflection: What is God trying to teach you in your current struggles?

Lesson 58: Letting Go of Bitterness

Scripture Reference: Ephesians 4:31

For Further Reflection: What bitterness are you carrying around? Ask God's forgiveness for holding onto it and His help in letting go of it.

Lesson 59: Believing and Not Doubting

Scripture References: Jeremiah 29:13; 33:3; Mark 9:24; Ephesians 6:16

For Further Reflection: What questions and doubts do you have? Have you talked to God about them? Will you believe God and trust Him?

Lesson 60: Submitting to God

Scripture References: Jeremiah 29:11; Luke 9:23; Romans 8:28; James 4:7

For Further Reflection: In what area of your life are you struggling to submit to God? Ask God for His help; then turn that area over to Him.

Lesson 61: God's Provision

Scripture Reference: Philippians 4:19

For Further Reflection: How has God provided for you? Are there any spending patterns that you need to change?

Lesson 62: Counting Your Blessings

Scripture References: Psalm 107:1; 1 Thessalonians 5:18

For Further Reflection: What are three things for which you are thankful today?

Lesson 63: Waiting on the Lord

Scripture References: Psalm 27:14; Ephesians 3:20

For Further Reflection: For what are you waiting? Are you trusting God during the wait?

Lesson 64: Peace that Passes Understanding

Scripture References: 2 Corinthians 10:5; Philippians 4:6–8; Colossians 3:1–2; Hebrews 12:2

For Further Reflection: On what do you fix your thoughts—God or your problems?

Lesson 65: Listening to Satan's Lies

Scripture References: Deuteronomy 7:6; Psalm 119:138,140,142,144; 139:14; 1 Corinthians 12:4–11; Ephesians 6:10–18

For Further Reflection: Are you listening to Satan's lies or are you clinging to God's truths?

Lesson 66: Negative Self-Talk

Scripture References: Genesis 1:27; Psalm 139:13–14; Colossians 3:12; 1 Peter 2:9

For Further Reflection: Do you love yourself or do you put yourself down?

Lesson 67: Complaining

Scripture References: Numbers 13–14; Psalm 118:24; Philippians 2:14–16

For Further Reflection: Do you grumble and complain, or do you live with an attitude of gratitude?

Lesson 68: All about God

Scripture References: Matthew 5:16; 1 Corinthians 10:31

For Further Reflection: Is your life pointing to God or is it pointing to you?

Lesson 69: Clothed with Humility

Scripture References: Philippians 2:3–8; 1 Peter 5:5–7

For Further Reflection: Are you clothed with humility?

Lesson 70: Walking by Faith

Scripture Reference: 2 Corinthians 5:7–9

For Further Reflection: Are you walking by faith or by sight?

Endnotes

Introduction

[1] *National Center for Health Statistics: http://www.cdc.gov/nchs/fastats/fertile.htm* (September 4, 2013).

Lesson 6

[1] Paris, Twila. "God Is in Control" *100 EZ Inspirational Favorites*. Word Music: Waco, TX, 1996.

Lesson 10

[1] Ball, Diane. "In His Time" *Maranatha! Music Praise Chorus Book*, 3rd edition. Word Maranatha: Nashville, TN, 1993.

Lesson 12

[1] Krippayne, Scott. "Sometimes He Calms the Storm" *Wild Imagination. Lyrics Mode: http://www.lyricsmode.com/lyrics/s/scott_krippayne/sometimes_he_calms_the_storm.html* (April 14, 2013).

Lesson 53

[1] McKinney, B. B. "Have Faith in God" *Baptist Hymnal*. Convention Press: Nashville, TN, 1975.

Lesson 62

[1] Oatman, Johnson, Jr. "Count Your Blessings" *Baptist Hymnal*. Convention Press: Nashville, TN, 1975.

CPSIA information can be obtained at www.ICGtesting.com
Printed in the USA
LVOW06s2107270614

392072LV00001B/3/P